# the way we talk now

COMMENTARIES ON

LANGUAGE AND CULTURE

*from NPR's "Fresh Air"*

GEOFFREY NUNBERG

Houghton Mifflin Company

*Boston   New York*

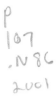

No part of this work may be reproduced or transmitted in any
form or by any means, electronic or mechanical, including photo-
copying and recording, or by any information storage or retrieval
system without the prior written permission of Houghton Mifflin
Company unless such copying is expressly permitted by federal
copyright law. Address inquiries to Reference Permissions,
Houghton Mifflin company, 222 Berkeley St. Boston, MA 02116.

Visit our website: www.houghtonmifflinbooks.com

*Library of Congress Cataloging-in-Publication Data*
Nunberg, Geoffrey, 1945-
    The way we talk now: commentaries on language and culture from
NPR's "Fresh air" / Geoffrey Nunberg.
        p. cm.
    ISBN 0-618-11602-8 — ISBN 0-618-11603-6
    1. Language and languages. I. Fresh air (Radio program) II. Title.

P107 .N86 2001
400—dc21
                                                      2001024797

MV 10 9 8 7 6 5 4 3 2 1
Book design by Melodie Wertelet
Manufactured in the United States of America

# Contents

## Politics of the English Language

## The Two R'S

## Technical Terms

## Business Talk

## Valediction

# Preface

Over the thirteen years that I've been doing language commentaries for the National Public Radio program *Fresh Air*, I've occasionally recorded several pieces at a time. So it happens now and then that I run into friends who say "I heard you on the radio yesterday" without my knowing which piece aired. When I ask which one they heard, it sometimes takes them a minute to remember; there will be an embarrassed pause, followed by something like "Gee, let me think — I was turning left off Folsom onto Ninth . . . ."

I can sympathize. That recession from consciousness is an inevitable effect of the way most of us listen to the radio nowadays, our minds darting nimbly between the program, the calls we have to make when we get to the office, and the jerk in the SUV who just cut us off. When we get out of the car, it can feel like waking up: we file away what we heard in the same part of the brain where dreams are stored.

But then, that's pretty much the way we hear most of the talk that comes at us. It lingers for a few seconds in short-term memory, and then it evanesces. Ten minutes later we can recall what we were told but not how. Even the strains and cracks of language escape our notice; like the incongruities of dreams, they're obvious only when we reflect on them in the light of day. And as with dreams, it can be hard to discern the work that talk is doing, over and above getting us from point A to point B.

The pieces collected here are efforts to snatch some insights from the torrent of our talk in the brief interval before it fades out of hearing. Taken together, the topics are a jumble, but that's probably a fair picture of our collective mind over the past decade: *PC . . . downsize . . . nigger . . . Luddite . . . community . . . yadda yadda . . . postmodern . . . Are you OK with that?* . . .

*virtual . . . Ebonics . . . chad . . . hackers . . . whatever!* Some of these are the keywords of our culture; others are as fleeting as the voices that come over the car radio. In either case, though, it's sometimes more interesting to sneak up on words rather than tackle them head-on. That's the way linguists like to work: we fasten on some inconspicuous detail of usage and worry it until a crack opens and we can glimpse the hurly-burly going on outside. And for these purposes it really isn't necessary to focus on the important words. You can do just as well prowling around the proletarian quarters of the vocabulary, where suffixes and interjections live out their ordinary lives. The more mundane the setting, the greater the pleasure you take in turning up some unexpected revelation; it's like happening on a Goya at a garage sale.

Those revealing minutiae can be compelling, precisely because we're normally unaware of them — they evoke the uncanny feeling we have when we realize that our unconscious has inadvertently given itself away. It doesn't take any special training or perspicacity to notice such things, once you get into the habit of cocking your ears for them. But it's useful to keep an open mind as well. I'm not one of those Panglossian linguists who think that everything happens for the best in our language. I hear a lot of talk that I am content to observe from the sidelines; for example, I personally prefer to call problems *problems* and to reserve the word *issue* for matters like universal health care. But I'm not comfortable with the style of criticism that calls attention to language only to deplore it. If you think you're smarter than the language, you're liable not to attend to what it's saying.

I've felt some qualms about publishing these radio pieces in their original form. The language of modern radio is more conversational than that of print, and the syntax is simpler — you learn to make your sentences shorter and to avoid lists and relative clauses. And the medium leaves its mark on the structure too, for instance in the way it encourages those perky final paragraphs that let your listeners know you're about to close. But most of the pieces were simply too topical or too ephemeral to justify my rewriting them as essays, and I finally decided to publish them pretty much as they were read.

Just after World War II, Max Beerbohm published a collection of his half-hour BBC radio broadcasts. The short preface began: "I fear that an apology should be made to any reader of the six broadcasts that form the greater part of this book. They were composed for the ears of listeners; and though of course a writer should always write not less for the ear than for the eye of the reader, he does not, in writing for the ear only, express himself in just the way that would be his if he were writing for the eye as well." When you read over Beerbohm's essays, though, it's hard to tell what he felt obliged to apologize for. The syntax and diction sound much the same as in his print essays, and there is no mistaking his dapper voice.

It may be that a contemporary writer has to make more concessions to the radio form than writers did back in Beerbohm's day, when people gathered after dinner to listen attentively to the evening broadcast over a console that had no preset buttons to turn to in the event of longueur. (When Beerbohm was getting ready to sign off, he could simply say, "Ladies and gentlemen, good night," without any summative throat-clearing — all well and good when you're broadcasting live at nine in the evening but not a feasible strategy when you're taping a piece that will run on different stations at all hours.) Even so, there's no question that Beerbohm was sincere in feeling he had to apologize for publishing his broadcasts as they were written. And I find some hope in realizing that the stylistic adjustments he made in writing for radio are not as evident to a reader as they were to him.

Over the years I've lost count of all the people who have suggested topics for radio pieces, forwarded me interesting material, or provided a fact or reference that allowed a piece to gleam with the luster of borrowed erudition. To them I'll have to extend a generic acknowledgment. But there are a few friends and colleagues with whom I conferred so frequently that they deserve special mention: Howard Bloch, Leo Braudy, Rachel Brownstein, Michelle Carter, Paul Duguid, Elisabeth Feldman, Linda Georgianna, Kathleen Hickey, Lauri Karttunen, John Lamping, Larry Masinter, Bob Newsom, Scott Parker, Joe Pickett, Ellen Prince, John Rickford, Hinrich Schuetze, Brian Smith, Tom Wasow, and Deborah Wolfe. Michelle Carter's indulgent support included reading over the manuscript of this book; thanks to her, I was able to improve some pieces that needed help and eliminate others that were past it. Katya Rice helped to organize the book and copy-edited the pieces with unfailing intelligence and attention to detail, undaunted by the grammatical and orthographic insouciance with which I had prepared these texts when I thought they were destined only for reading aloud. Jacquelyn Pope and Wade Ostrowski at Houghton Mifflin made final adjustments to the text. I owe thanks, too, to Joe Pickett and Marge Berube of Houghton Mifflin, and to my agent, Joe Spieler, for seeing that the project got safely off the launching pad.

These pieces could not have appeared without the efforts of the staff of *Fresh Air* and its executive producer, Danny Miller, who manage week in and week out to turn out a show of consistently high quality. I am especially grateful to Phyllis Myers and Naomi Person, the producers I've worked with over the years; I thank them for their friendship, for their frequent encouragement ("Whaddya got for us this week?"), and for patiently teaching me how to write for radio. And needless to say, I am immensely grateful to Terry Gross for creating a valued space in the culture and allowing me to be a part of it.

Finally, it will be obvious to anyone who reads through this collection that I owe a special debt to Sophie Nunberg, who began to inspire pieces shortly after she was born, and whose subsequent contributions to my linguistic understanding are frequently documented in these pages.

All of these pieces were originally broadcast on *Fresh Air*, except for "Slides Rule," which appeared in *Fortune*; "Come Together, Right Now," which appeared under the title "Convergence" in *Forbes ASAP*; "Chad Row," which appeared in the *San Jose Mercury-News*; and "Shall Game," which appeared in *California Lawyer*.

# the passing scene

# The Choice of Sophie {1989}

**A**s soon as we knew it was going to be a girl, we started looking for a name in earnest. Men's names are like men's ties: there are only about six of them, and you run into the same ones over and over again. The five most popular boys' names in 1925 were Robert, John, William, James, and Charles; in 1950, Robert, Michael, James, John, and David; in 1970, Michael, Robert, David, James, and John. All solid, unimaginative stuff. It's only in the last few years that boys' names have begun to bend to the winds of fashion. In 1982 the most popular names were Michael, Christopher, Matthew, David, and in fifth position Jason, a name that didn't even make the top fifty ten years earlier. But girls' names are traditionally much more subject to caprice. In 1925 the top five were Mary, Barbara, Dorothy, Betty, and Ruth. In 1970 they were Michelle, Jennifer, Kimberly, Lisa, and Tracy, with Mary down at number fifteen. And by 1982 the top five were Jennifer, Sarah, Nicole, Jessica, and Katherine. Mary had fallen all the way to number thirty-one, behind Megan, Erin, and Crystal. Naming a girl child is like buying her a trousseau twenty years in advance.

I wanted something vaguely old-fashioned and Middle European, sort of a feminine version of Max or Emil, which would sidle up nicely to Nunberg. But my wife is French, and wanted something that worked in that language as well. She vetoed Louise and Paula, which was probably just as well. I told her that Géraldine might be all very well in French but that it was out of the question in America for as long as there are people alive who remember Flip Wilson. We toyed with Isabelle and

Adèle, then hit on Sophie, which seemed an ideal solution. So-phie for New World, So-*phie* for the Old.

I had the first inkling that there might be a problem when my friend Greg was out visiting from New York. Greg is my pipeline to the cutting edge: he was listening to Zydeco and eating arugula when Jimmy Carter was president. He asked me if we had a name for the baby yet; then before I could answer he said, "Wait, don't tell me. You're going to call her Sophie." I was taken aback, to put it mildly. "How'd you guess *that*?" "Look," he said, "these things are in the air. You could be in a cave in Alaska for ten years, and then your wife gets pregnant and you say, 'I've got it — we'll call the kid Blair!'" I tried to put this out of my mind, but it made me nervous. And then just two weeks before the baby was due, we were watching an epi-sode of *Thirtysomething* where one of the characters had gotten herself a cat and named *it* Sophie.

I began to fear that we had hit upon the Jennifer of the 90s. Strange, the way the collective mind works. Here are all these prospective parents poring over name books while they practice their breathing. They've been ruled by language all their lives, constrained to call things by the names that other people gave them. Now they have the opportunity to label one little bundle of reality with whatever name strikes their fancy, and as if by magic they all stop on the same page.

I thought about what it would be like in nursery school, with two or three other Sophies, a Lindsay and a Chelsea, and a clutch of Chloës and Zoës with diereses dancing over their curls. And what would happen forty years later? Was Sophie going to be one of those names that are so tied to a particular decade that they wind up as markers of dowdy middle age, like Mildred, Ethel, and Flo?

We went with the name anyway. Even if it turns out to be

trendy, she'll make it her own. You only have to look at her to know that. After all, Doris Day is no ordinary Doris, and Audrey Hepburn makes you rethink Audrey. And whatever you associate with Marilyn, you make at least one exception. Sophie Nunberg. You heard it here first.

# Vietnamese for Travelers    {1989}

Over the years, I must have collected about twenty of those little books that offer to teach "useful phrases for the traveler" in one language or another. It's a captivating genre, which encapsulates all of the fond faith of travel planning. The guides try to offer pat phrases for any eventuality, including some that are pretty implausible. The classic example is a nineteenth-century guide for French tourists in England that offered the sentence "Our coachman has been struck by lightning." Or take this one, from a book called *French Without Toil*: "That's true, the lyrics are cretinous, but the melody is agreeable." I've kept this sentence on the tip of my tongue over the years I have been visiting France, but I haven't been able to work it into a conversation.

But even phrases that sound at first as if they might come in handy turn out to have not much use in daily life. For example, the Dover guide called *Say It in Spanish* provides the sentence "Here is the check for my trunk." I like the sound of that one; I once spent a day walking around Seville repeating it like a mantra: "Ah-*kee tyay*-nay oos-*ted* el ta-*lohn* day mee ba-*ool*." But it's not something I have ever wanted to say in earnest in Spanish or any other language, and I don't think many other travelers have needed that one, either. You'd not only have to have a trunk and leave it at the railroad station checkroom, but you'd have to be reckless enough to hand the claim ticket to a complete stranger who knew no English. On the other hand, you can scour these books in vain for the phrases that you actually do find yourself needing when you are abroad, even simple things like "It's not leaking on that side" or "You might have told us about the band practice when we checked in."

A friend of mine recently sent me what has to be the most

poignant example of this genre. It is a small, khaki-colored handbook of Vietnamese phrases which was published by the Department of the Army in 1962 for issue to U.S. personnel in South Vietnam. At the time the Vietnamese involvement was still being described as a "counterinsurgency operation." There were four or five thousand U.S. advisors there, and the Pentagon was arguing that another couple of thousand would suffice to turn the tide of the war. Here are several phrases drawn from the first section, on "initial encounters with locals":

> Hello. I am an American officer who seeks friends to assist in fighting the enemy. Hide my parachute.
>
> We heard about your (1) patriotic work (2) sufferings (3) willingness to cooperate.
>
> Does anyone here have relatives in the U.S.?
>
> Sit down. Have a cigarette. Have a chocolate.

From there the phrasebook provides questions to determine what it calls the "potential of locals for organization of guerrilla units," with items like:

> Do the people here (1) hate (2) like (3) fear (1) the regime (2) violence (3) the Soviets?
>
> Do they believe in the annihilation of Bolshevism?
>
> Would they sacrifice their lives for U.S. troops?

Like *Say It in Spanish*, the book makes for a good cautionary tale about the difficulty of anticipating everything that might befall you when you embark on a foreign adventure:

> We are here to help in the struggle on the side of (1) the free world (2) the U.S. (3) the Allies (4) freedom (5) God.
>
> Thank you for your cooperation. God bless you. Now hurry. So long.

# You Know

I suppose the point of all language criticism is to read monumental consequences in trivial derelictions. But I can't think of anyplace where the disproportion is as great as in the abuse that critics have heaped on the little phrase *you know*. Not long ago Senator Robert Byrd actually delivered a speech on the floor of the Senate deploring the expanding use of the expression: "The phrase betrays a mind whose thoughts are so disorganized as to be unutterable — a mind in neutral gear connected to a tongue stuck in overdrive."

Of course, there are *you know*s and *you know*s, and most of them are unquestionably useful linguistic citizens. There's the *you know* of self-revelation, as in "You know, I've never engaged in this kind of thing before." There's the *you know* of remonstrance, as in "You know, you're not the only one with angst." And there's the *you know* that announces a sudden insight, as in "You know, these round things would go great with cream cheese and lox." But the *you know* that bothers critics is something else again. It's the one that you stick in the middle of a sentence when words fail you and you want to throw yourself on the mercy of the context: "Oh, but George is, you know, kind of weird about opera" — as if to say, "I'm not putting this with as much accuracy as precise communication might require, but I'm counting on you to cut me a little slack here."

Used in moderation, it's a harmless enough little noise. And sometimes it can be a useful way of nodding to the communion of conversation, a reminder that friends don't expect friends to spell everything out for them. It's true that some people overdo this in an annoying way, and it does seem as if a lot of them are teenagers. But it's not clear why the problem should be worth twenty minutes on C-SPAN, or why Edwin Newman should call *you know* "one of the most far-reaching and depressing developments of our time" — quite a claim to make in an age that has given us linguistic innovations like *incentivize* and *ethnic cleansing.*

As it happens, there's nothing particularly new about the phrase; Americans have probably been using it for at least a century and a half. It's true that you don't run across it much in Melville or James, but it isn't the kind of phrase that writers would have set down in the cleaned-up dialogue of novels. If you went strictly by the literary evidence, you'd probably conclude that nobody ever said *um* before 1947. Still, it's likely that *you know* was used as much in nineteenth-century conversation as it is today.

Anyway, before it was *you know* it was something else. People have always had their conversational tics and twitches, but critics didn't use to take public notice of this kind of language. For all we know, Benjamin Disraeli was positively phobic about the overuse of *I say*; but he would never have risen in the House of Commons to deliver a speech about it.

What's different now is that conversation isn't a private affair anymore — it has become the chief vehicle of entertainment and public information. We have become a society of o-verhearers. From dawn to midnight, you can spend every minute of the day listening to other people schmooze. They're schmoozing with Phil and Oprah, with Larry King, with Bill Moyers, with Jay and Arsenio. They're schmoozing with each other on the local news, on *McNeil-Lehrer*, on *The Washington Gang.* And the conversation of these shows is a strange new form of discourse. It's an intimate colloquy between people who may never have met before, where the real audience is acknowledged only in the third person. "Well, Barbara, your viewers might not realize...."

In this simulated intimacy there is no real common ground

to appeal to and no dispensation to be vague. Fillers like *you know* that pass unnoticed in ordinary conversation can suddenly strike us as oddly inappropriate. Professional interviewers and talk-show hosts appreciate this, of course. They may use a *you know* now and again, but always with a certain amount of artifice. It's a way of implying intimacy without really being intimate, the way the set of *Good Morning America* is supposed to imply a living room without actually being one. But you can see how the guests or the callers might not get this right, how they might start talking to the host as if they were alone with someone they really *were* on a first-name basis with: "Yeah, but Larry, it's like lots of people are, you know, out of work."

Most of these people wouldn't be so quick to use *you know* if they were at a job interview. That's what's really disturbing about hearing the expression over the air: you realize just how credible the manufactured intimacy of television can be, to the point where people have trouble telling who their real friends are anymore.

# Yesss, Indeed!   {1995}

Sophie's almost five now, back in the States after a year and a half in France. Right now her English is still larded with Gallicisms. She sometimes puts the adjective after the noun, as in "Poppa, you give me the popsicle red." And she says things like "I wanna look television," which comes from translating the French verb *regarder* literally. It will all pass within a couple of months, now that she's back in an American school. But right now it gives her a winsome quality, kind of like a French Dondi. And it makes for striking moments when every once in a while she opens her mouth and delivers herself of a chunk of pure adolescent Americana. The other day I told her to put on her sweater and she said, "No way, José." And later we were having an argument about whether to rent her a video, and when I finally gave in, she threw both her fists in the air and said, "Yesss!" I asked her, "Sophie, what does that mean, *yesss?*" And she said, "*En anglais* you say that when you win."

Of course I know where she got it. She got it from looking television. It's part of the language of postmodern childhood, if that isn't a contradiction in terms. Sebastian the crab says it in *The Little Mermaid* after he swings a block and tackle into the cook who's chasing him and knocks out all the cook's teeth. Aladdin says it in *The Return of Jafar*. You see kids saying it all the time in commercials for video-game players and candy bars.

I've heard different theories about where this *yesss* business started. One friend of mine is sure it's a Bill Murray–*Saturday Night Live* thing, and other people have told me it's a Michael J. Fox thing or an Arsenio Hall thing. My own guess is that it was started by Marv Alpert, the New York Knicks announcer.

But actually I don't know that it matters much just which shipment of fruit this bug came in with. The important thing is that it was a TV thing, and that it started to become popular in the mid-80s, around the same time as the *thing* thing did. (That, by the way, is another expression that has worked its way into the cartoons, and it's probably only a matter of time before Sophie picks it up as well: "You don't understand, Poppa. It's a kid thing.")

So what is this *yesss* business, anyway? It's like a cry of triumph, except that it isn't much of a cry, not like "Olé!" or "Hooray" or "Yahoo" or "Banzai!" You say it with a hiss, not a yell, and without ever opening your teeth. In fact it must be one of the only triumphant exclamations in the world that end in a consonant. And it's usually uttered after the fact or at a remove from the action. It's what a sitcom adolescent says when he has hung up the phone after getting a date, or what his dad says after he's walked out of his boss's office with a raise. It makes you into a spectator of your own triumph, like Marv Alpert watching Earl the Pearl sink a jumper: "Monroe...yesss!"

That's where the expression gets its ironic charm, particularly in the mouths of comics like Bill Murray or Arsenio Hall who make a shtick out of maintaining a distance from the tumult of their inner life. And you can see why it would have a lot of appeal for adolescents who are struggling to keep their cool in the midst of a hormonal Beirut. But it's a little disconcerting to hear it from those precociously hip eight-year-olds in the video-game commercials.

Of course Sophie is still a few years away from grasping the notion of ironic detachment. When we got to the video store that day she rushed to the cartoon rack to pull down a Flintstones tape. "Poppa, we get this one. Yabba dabba doo!"

# Look–See  {1994}

I drive home from Palo Alto to San Francisco on Route 280. It's a beautiful road; it winds up the middle of the Peninsula with hills and lakes on one side and glimpses of the bay five miles away on the other. Usually it's the only time of the day I get to relax and think about anything for more than five minutes at a stretch. Except that on this particular day I wasn't interested in the view, and everything that was coming to mind was something that I really didn't want to think about — a problem with a real estate escrow, a defective computer monitor I couldn't get the dealer to replace. You don't want to know.

My cassette player was broken and I was in the part of the drive where it's hard to pull in any music stations. I for sure wasn't interested in listening to NPR in that kind of mood; it's like newzak.

I started to punch up the AM stations. On the sports talk show they were talking about the Warriors, which only made me more irritated. Don't get me started on the Warriors. I pushed the SCAN button and the radio started lurching up the band, and then I heard a man's voice saying, "You see, my friend...." That's all it took, just "You see, my friend...," and I knew I was right where I needed to be, at one of those stations that's just for us angry white guys.

This is the only place on radio where they call people "my friend." It's the way you talk to somebody when you're trying to clue him in on something: "Wake up and smell the roses, my friend." For that matter, they don't say "See..." that way on FM talk shows — I mean the kind of "See" that means, "Let me wise you up about this." As in "See, that's exactly what Bill Clinton wants you to think." Or, "You see, those people don't want to learn English." It's the expression you use when you think that everything has a hidden explanation. It's not at all like "Look," which is what you say when you're trying to resolve a disagreement. As in "Look, I'll give you that the Warriors are in trouble all over, but they still could use a number two guard."

People weren't saying "Look" much on the show I was listening to. Maybe there weren't many disagreements, or maybe nobody really cared about resolving them. It was more of an exercise in the pure syntax of indignation. The way I was feeling, I could understand this perfectly. It didn't have anything to do with politics. You can be ticked off at Janet Reno and the BATF or you can be ticked off at the hosts and the callers. Either way, you get an agreeable buzz of irritation on. You feel a sense of community with a great brotherhood of ticked-off white guys all over the country, all listening to the radio and muttering to themselves.

I listened to the the ads for gold coins and vocabulary-building cassette tapes. They did a station ID that said the station was the place that still cared about the working stiff. Right, I thought, I'm both of those.

I was getting the hang of the syntax. A guy called in with a story about how liberal photographers are always using motor drives and catching conservative politicians with their mouths open. I wasn't sure what the point was. I don't think the radio host got it either, but he didn't pursue it. Whatever it was, it probably fit in somewhere. "I hear you," he said. "Isn't that always the way?" "That's always the way," the guy said. "You keep up the good work, now." I had this urge to call the show on the line they reserve for cellular phones. "Let's go to Geoff on the car phone from the Peninsula. What's your mind, Geoff?" I'd tell him about the problem I was having with my monitor. Then he'd say, "See, that dealer has no intention of replacing that monitor." "Right," I'd tell him, "that's how I had it figured. Isn't that always the way?" He'd say, "You got it, my friend — that's always the way." "Well, thanks," I'd say. "Hey, you're doing a great job there."

Enough already. When I crossed Route 92 I pushed the button on the radio; I could pick up the jazz station now. I started to feel better. On my left the sun was slipping behind the fog that was pouring over the ridge line. I looked, I saw.

# The N–Word   {1995}

Just after the O.J. verdict was announced, I was talking with a Stanford colleague, a Caribbean-born African-American. He told me about an image he'd seen on TV the night before, a bit of spray-painted graffiti in L.A. that said THE NIGGER DID IT. "You know," he said, "I've been living in this country for thirty years, and I swear I've never seen or heard that word used in public so much as in the past few months."

Thirty years sounded just about right. I recall watching the early episodes of Henry Hampton's *Eyes on the Prize* series on PBS a couple of years ago and being struck at how unselfconscious a lot of white people seemed to be about using the word *nigger* in televised interviews back in the 50s and early 60s. It was only in the following years that this sort of language came to seem crude, particularly among middle-class suburban whites. They had already put the beltways between themselves and inner-city blacks, and now they wanted to put a little linguistic space between themselves and the rednecks in Mayberry, RFD. And politicians rapidly learned that they didn't have to use words like *nigger* to make their point — they could just talk about welfare queens, quotas, or "the element." I don't know that any of it made for a kinder, gentler nation, but it made for a slightly subtler one.

But now the word seems to be all over the place again. I suppose the Simpson trial is part of the reason, but that isn't the whole of it. There was a telling example on Larry King a couple of weeks ago. Robert Novak was the guest host and Jesse Helms was the guest, and somebody called in from Alabama and said, "Mr. Helms, I know this might not be politically correct to say these days, but I just think that you should get a Nobel Peace

Prize for everything you've done to help keep down the niggers." The two men laughed nervously, and then Novak said, "That was the bad word, that was politically incorrect. We don't really condone that kind of language, though, do we?" And Helms agreed but added that "Mark Twain used it." Somehow neither of them got around to saying anything about the content of the caller's remarks, like suggesting that maybe keeping down the niggers wasn't the sort of thing they ought to award the Nobel Peace Prize for.

It's true that most middle-class whites are uncomfortable when they hear the word *nigger* used on Larry King or on tapes played in open court. But it isn't clear whether Mark Fuhrman's problem was that he came off as a racist or that he came off as a redneck racist. Certainly there are a lot of whites who tend to think of racial slurs on the model of ordinary profanities — words we don't use in public. There was a suggestion of this in the coy way the press and witnesses kept referring to the epithet in question as "the *n*-word." That's the formula we always use for the other words which we teach our children not to say in polite conversation, and which they learn to take a naughty pleasure in saying in private. The repression was simmering for a long time, and now the cork has popped. The verdict is in, and the gloves are off.

# Some Pig! {1995}

It wasn't a speech code, exactly, more like a bit of usage advice. The idea was to get Stanford administrators and faculty to speak with one voice in promoting the university and setting it apart from its rivals. To this end Terry Shepherd, the university's director of communications, issued a strategic plan that included a single list of adjectives for people to use when they talked about the place. There were six of them in all: *challenging, western, incomparable, boundless, stunning,* and *vibrant.* Shepherd explained the list by saying, "If we all use the same terms, Stanford would come to mean the same things to people."

It all seems fair enough to me. I don't know that Stanford is any more challenging or incomparable than Yale or the University of Chicago, but it's for sure more western. And it's certainly more vibrant than those other schools, which are sitting a thousand miles or more from the nearest major fault line.

According to Stanford president Gerhard Caspar, the idea for the list was originally proposed by some university trustees who come from the business world. It's an approach that has worked very nicely for corporations. And a few years ago Newt Gingrich showed how effective it can be as a political strategy when he had GOPAC issue a list of sixty-four adjectives for Republican candidates to memorize and use to describe themselves and their opponents.

But when Stanford's list was leaked to the press, the faculty proved to be deficient in the team spirit that it takes to put this sort of approach over the top. Academics tend to have the sense that they ought to be allowed to make up their own words. There was a heated meeting of the faculty senate, and other adjectives began to fill the air — words like *anti-intellectual, va-*

*pid,* and *insulting.* The president rapidly decided to scrap the plan.

I can certainly understand the point of view of the faculty, but I have to say I feel some sympathy for the communications people too. It's a profession that gets no respect, which is probably why they keep changing their job description every ten years or so to spruce up their image. First they were press agents, and then they were public relations people, and now they're in communications. People heap abuse on them all the same.

But you have to give them at least this: there's no one else who has such devotion to the powers of language. The point came home to me the other night when my daughter and I were reading *Charlotte's Web.* It's a book that everybody loves, of course, but it must have a special place in the hearts of the communications folks. Here's this creepy little creature feeding on flies in a corner of the barn and trying to save a pig from slaughter. So she gets a rat to pick some clippings out of the garbage, and then she spins a gossamer of words out of her rear, and all of a sudden everyone's looking at the pigsty with new eyes. It's a fine demonstration of the power of language to transform our perceptions of the world. Stanford University — Some Pig!

# A Few of My Favorite Words   {1995}

There was a story in the *Wall Street Journal* the other day about a Texas dentist who's building a one-hundred-ten-foot-tall catapult with the aim of hurling a Buick two hundred fifty yards through the air. He chose the Buick because it's heavy and because he likes its name. Well, Buick *is* a great name. Nobody would build a siege engine to throw something called a Taurus or an Altima around. It shows what lengths some people will go to out of the pure love of words.

The story reminded me of Bernard Pivot, the Barbara Walters of French literature. For the past twenty years or so Pivot has been hosting a prime-time literary interview show that consistently outdraws *Dallas* or *Dynasty* or whatever the other stations throw up against it. One of the stock questions he always throws at writers is "What's your favorite word?" The last time I caught Pivot, his guests were William Styron, who was speaking through an interpreter, and some politician who'd just written a novel. When Pivot asked Styron the question, he seemed at a bit of a loss and launched into a windy evasion, "Well, you know, asking a writer to choose a favorite word is like asking a parent to choose a favorite child." Pivot had obviously heard this sort of thing before and cut Styron off. *Merci*, he said, and moved on to the politician. *He* of course had seen the show many times and was ready for the question. *La paix*, he said right off — "peace." Pivot arched his eyebrows to show he clearly didn't think a lot of that answer, either. He was right, too. I mean, peace may be a wonderful concept, but it's not much of a word, not in French or in English. Now, maybe *peas* . . .

It's not an easy question. Some people try to give you what

they think are beautiful-sounding words, like *pearl*, or *willow*, or *autumn*. But that's always a tricky business, because you're never sure how much your impression of the sound is colored by the meaning. Max Beerbohm once asked a friend, "Do you not think that *ermine* is among the most beautiful-sounding words in the language?" "Oh, to be sure," his friend replied. And Beerbohm said, "Well, what about *vermin*?" On the other hand, there are some absolutely gorgeous-sounding words that we tend to overlook because their meanings are repellent. Take *melanoma*. A beautiful word; you want it to be the name of a tropical wind instead of a tumor. You think of something out of a Carmen Miranda song: "Smell the tropical aroma / Carried on the melanoma." Actually a lot of medical words have that feeling — like *diarrhea*. What a waste of fine syllables *that* is.

What we're looking for isn't sound or meaning alone but the happy wedding of the two. My daughter understood that right off when I asked her what her favorite word was. "Knuckle-head," she said without missing a beat, as if she'd been thinking about it all afternoon.

I don't think I could be that decisive. I'm not even sure what part of speech I'd start with. I used to have a thing about the preposition *athwart*, because I always liked the line from *Romeo and Juliet* about how the queen of the fairies gallops "athwart men's noses as they lie asleep." But now all of a sudden *athwart*'s gotten popular again. You can't throw a rock without hitting a sentence like "Modern Yugoslavia sat athwart the fault lines of European history" or "He sets himself athwart the tide of conventional wisdom." They've ruined *athwart*. If it were a girl's name it would be Ashley.

Maybe I'd pick a verb. *Entitle. Wallop.* Or how about *bamboozle*? You tell foreigners about *bamboozle*, they always think it's a much more serious offense than it is. Or *peruse*. A lot of people like *peruse*. Nobody's sure exactly what it means, but people say it anyway because they like the sound of it. It gives us a nice noun, too, with vaguely Yiddish echoes: "I enclose these documents for your perusal."

Or adjectives. I have a weakness for the ones that go after the noun. Like *galore*. Or better yet, *akimbo*. I always take a certain pleasure in working this into a conversation: "Oh nothing, I'm just sitting here, you know, akimbo." It's actually a good old Anglo-Saxon word, but it has this nice exotic lilt about it. *Akimbo!*— that's what I'm going to call my blockbuster novel, when I get around to writing it.

In the end, though, I suppose you have to choose a noun. If Bernard Pivot ever asks me, I'll pick *lap*. That evanescent body part which no other language has a name for. The anagram of *alp*, the reverse of *pal*. That's a noun to make you want to hurl a couple of thousand pounds of metal in the air.

# Rex Ipse   {1995}

*Winnie Ille Pu* has to be one of the most unlikely literary successes of modern times. It was a 1960 version of the Pooh stories translated into Latin by a European Bach scholar living in Brazil, the first foreign-language book ever to hit the *New York Times* bestseller lists.

The book has always bothered me. *Winnie-the-Pooh* is precious enough in English, and translating it into Latin invests that language with entirely the wrong sort of nostalgia. If we're going to have a commercial success in Latin, I'd much prefer that it be something along the lines of the CD I just received in the mail from a Finnish friend. It's the work of a man named Jukka Ammondt, an amateur singer and professor of literature at the University of Jyvaskala in Finland. As Ammondt tells the story, he was going through a period of intense depression when Elvis Presley came to him in a dream and told him to record his songs in Latin. (This seems to be a recurring Finnish theme — there's that scene in the Finnish-American director Jim Jarmusch's *Mystery Train* where the ghost of Elvis makes an appearance to an Italian woman in a Memphis hotel room.) In any event, Ammondt went to a colleague from the classics department and they collaborated on a CD called *The Legend Lives Forever.*

Ammondt doesn't try to translate any of Elvis's early rockers, which is probably just as well. I could go to my grave very happily without knowing what "You Ain't Nothin but a Hound Dog" sounds like in Latin. Instead he concentrates on ballads, particularly the Mediterranean sort of material that Elvis started to perform in the 60s, songs like "I Can't Help Falling in Love with You," "Impossible," and "It's Now or Never" — or as it goes in Latin, "Nunc Hic aut Numquam."

It's a kind of music that appeals to Finnish sensibilities (bear in mind that Finland is the tango capital of Europe), and actually it may have been the music that Elvis liked best too. When he was growing up, after all, the big vocalists were all those Italian-American singers like Tony Martin, Dean Martin, Jerry Vale, and Julius LaRosa. Peter Guralnick reports in his recent biography that Elvis had a big collection of Mario Lanza records when he was in his teens. And "It's Now or Never" was just a version of "O Sole Mio," which Tony Martin had had a hit with in 1950 under the title "There's No Tomorrow," and "Surrender" was just an English version of the Italian song "Come Back to Sorrento." I suppose you could argue that the whole rock 'n' roll interlude of the late 50s was only a digression for Elvis on the way to realizing his true ambition of becoming an Italian lounge singer.

It shouldn't be surprising that material first written in Italian should work fine in Latin, and yet it takes you aback a bit. We don't think of Latin as sounding so...well, so Latin. People always talk about Latin as this enormously logical and dignified language, the language of law and philosophy, the perfect instrument for inculcating mental discipline in generations of schoolboys before we all went soft and permissive. We think of it as having lots of genders but no sex. When you look at the rows of Roman busts in the Louvre or the Villa Borghese, it doesn't occur to you that these people even *had* pelvises. But of course that's a conception of Latin that has less to do with Catullus than with *Brideshead Revisited* — all those upper-class Englishmen sloshing around their country houses reciting Latin tags to their teddy bears. That's why *Winnie Ille Pu* was such a great success, I suppose: it turned Latin into a dialect of Edwardian English. But we should bear in mind that if the Latin poets were alive they'd be much bigger fans of

Elvis than of A. A. Milne — and who knows, maybe vice versa as well. It's too bad the CD doesn't include a Latin version of Elvis's great tribute to Virgil, "Aeneid Your Love Tonight."

# An Interjection for the Age   {1997}

I was talking to a young woman I know who had just returned from Burning Man, the neo-bohemian festival that's held every Labor Day weekend in the desert northeast of Reno. What was it like, I asked her, a Gen-X Woodstock? No, she told me, not a bit—this is post-counterculture. They're people who work at Charles Schwab and Yahoo!; a group from Intel came in a fleet of RVs. People walked around naked in the sun, or cruised the playa in beds rigged with sails and battery-powered recliner couches. There was nude croquet, an alien-abduction camp, and a huge script neon *W* that someone had rigged up on the top of a pole. I asked her what the *W* was for. "Well, what else could it be?" she said, and made her hands into a *W*, with her index fingers raised and her thumbs touching. "What-*ever*." It allayed any misgivings I might have had about not going to the festival myself. I mean, if you had to ask what the *W* stood for, you probably didn't belong there.

I have to admit, though, that that big *W* was a perfect totem for the last decade of the century. There's a funny thing about slang—it isn't just the words that change from one generation to the next, but the parts of speech. The language of the 60s had all those adjectives that described the various states of altered being: *far out, groovy, out of sight, funky, heavy, bummed.* The 70s and early 80s were the golden age of adverbs, with a dozen or more ways of saying "very." Everything was "mondo fine" or "seriously fresh," "way tired" or "totally to the curb." Or if you didn't get the adverb in at the beginning of the noun phrase you could always exit with one of those intensifier suffixes like "to the max" or "up the yin-yang." But over the past ten years or so the action's been in the interjections, the little particles that people use to comment on the passing conversational scene. What stands out when I roll the tape of 90s chatter is all these voices snapping pithy retorts. Excuse me. Duh. Hell-*o*? As *if*. Not even. Don't go there. *Not!*

It's true that a lot of these have been pretty short-lived. That *Wayne's World* "not!" was already passing out of use by the time the tape of the movie was being taken out of the "current" racks of the video stores, and not a minute too soon. But a few of these items seem to have legs, like that *whatever* that signals your sublime indifference to what your interlocutor is trying to say to you. Watching TV the other night I heard it three times, first in an MTV ad, then on *Ally McBeal*, then finally on *Suddenly Susan*. "I'll just go freshen my drink," says a guy chatting up a woman at a cocktail party. She rolls her eyes: "Whatever."

Of course every age has had its slang interjections. The one word that America has given to more languages than any other, after all, is the affirmative particle *OK*. The 50s had *solid*, the 60s had *far out*, the 70s saw the efflorescence of *Yo!* But those were all upbeat comments. This is the first age to focus exclusively on the noises of cynicism and ennui. You think of the refrain from the Kurt Cobain song "Smells Like Teen Spirit," which Nirvana made a miniature anthem for the decade: "Oh well, whatever, never mind."

It's not surprising that the survivors of Woodstock would find this a little wanting in warmth. What were the hippies about, after all, if not how far you could take good old American niceness if you set about it with single-minded intensity? On the other hand, it's an understandable reaction to the other linguistic excesses of recent years. It's no wonder that one of the emblematic figures of the age is the disaffected adolescent girl of *Beetlejuice, Heathers, Clueless*, or the MTV cartoon show *Daria*. You listen to the pumped-up beamer enthusiasm of modern corporate prose and it makes you feel like an adolescent girl yourself; it seems as if there's no possible response but sardonic deadpan. The other day I got a message thanking me for talking to some corporate advertising people. "In the debrief," it said, "it was clear that our future advertising directions had been positively challenged, and that they clearly harnessed a profound input." For the first time in my life I felt a "whatever" rising to my lips.

You can say this for *whatever*: it opens the way to new sensibilities. I wouldn't say that the word is ironic; it doesn't have the self-mockery or the underlying moral note that irony requires. But to take a throwaway tag that people say as if they had barely enough breath to get it out and erect it in neon fifty feet over the desert floor — that's real wit. And wit, after all, is something that was pretty thin on the ground at Yasgur's Farm.

# The Last Post   {1997}

**W**e used to know what modernism was, or at least *when* it was. It had to do with Picasso, Stravinsky, Mies Van Der Rohe, and Virginia Woolf. But at some point since then the period started to roll backwards. People began saying that modernism started seventy years earlier with Flaubert and Bentham, or they put it back with Diderot and Condorcet in the eighteenth century (which, by the way, has itself been redefined so that now it begins around 1660). Or earlier still. A couple of years ago people stopped talking about the Renaissance and started calling it the early modern period. It's hard to tell where it's all going to end, or rather where it will begin. I asked a medievalist friend, "OK, so who's the last premodern? Chaucer?" "Chaucer!" she said. "Oh, no—he's a remarkably modern figure." "Then how about William the Conqueror?" I asked. "Well," she said, "maybe before he crossed the Channel."

I suspect that one reason for this period creep is that the longer the modern age is, the greater the crash it makes when it goes down. Depending on where they're coming from, critics and philosophers locate the symbolic end of the modernist period at different moments—the appearance of Philip Johnson's AT&T Building in New York; the publication of Roland Barthes's *S/Z*; the first Steve Martin album, the one where he's wearing an arrow on his head. Whatever the date, though, everybody seems certain that modernity is a thing of the past, along with all its cultural fellow travelers: the narrative is unraveled, the author is dead, the Enlightenment project is toast, and history is history.

Of course people in every age like to think of themselves as living a millennial moment. Seventy-five years ago Marinetti was proclaiming that "we stand on the high peak between the ages," and you can find people saying more or less the same thing in every period going back to Hesiod. Still, it isn't every generation that gets to live at the brink of an honest-to-God millennium. And I don't know that any other age has thought of the Zeitgeist in such an exclusively retrospective way. People don't say "from now on," only "never again." Hence the passion for that prefix *post–*. We are postmodern, posthumanist, post-industrial, postliberal, post-Christian, post-structuralist, postfeminist, postcolonial. A writer in *The American Scholar* not long ago announced that we had entered the age of postculturalism. I have this image of everybody shuffling backwards toward the millennium under a banner that bears the device BEEN THERE, DONE THAT.

All these words with *post–* and *neo–* prefixes — it's as if we ran out of language all of a sudden, so there's nothing for it but to recycle the old words with new parts tacked on. But that's the mark of the postmodern. As Frederick Jameson pointed out, it's all pastiche, old signs in new bottles — Portman hotel lobbies, the Plymouth Prowler, neodisco, Blue Velvet, Combustible Edison. It can be a subtle business even trying to figure out what time it is. As *Wired* explained: "A modernist always wore a tie with a jacket; a postmodernist throws a well-tailored jacket over a T-shirt." It's the "well-tailored" that brings me up short: here is this epochal shift in the basic condition of being, and you have to have an eye for a lapel even to recognize that it has taken place.

It's as if all times are present at once — the effect that the post-structuralist theorists describe as the "always already there." Or maybe it's just that people have gotten a little confused about prefixes. You have the feeling that *post–* doesn't really mean "after" anymore; now it means something closer to "once more without feeling." For that matter, we're using the prefix *pre—* in new ways, too. People talk about preowned cars and preapproved loans; they announce preboarding and there are already people getting on the plane.

# As a Cigarette Should  {1997}

The year was 1954. The top-rated TV show was *I Love Lucy*, sponsored by Philip Morris, and close behind was *Your Hit Parade*, sponsored by Lucky Strikes, whose "Be Happy, Go Lucky" jingle had won *TV Guide*'s award for commercial of the year. And Otto Pritchard, a Pittsburgh carpenter with lung cancer, filed the first liability suit against a tobacco company.

In that year R. J. Reynolds introduced the new brand Winston, which unlike other filter cigarettes stressed taste rather than health. Reynolds ran a singing commercial with the tagline "Winston tastes good like a cigarette should." *Like* instead of *as* — as grammatical sins go it was pretty venial, but the purists went to the mattresses over it. One critic called it "belligerent illiteracy"; another suggested that the writer who came up with the ad should be jailed. The Winston people were delighted with all the free publicity. They capitalized on the controversy in a new campaign that featured the slogan "What do you want, good grammar or good taste?" Soon after that Tareyton got in on the act with a campaign headed "Us Tareyton smokers would rather fight than switch," and the whole dance went round again over pronouns.

It was a curious episode. It certainly wasn't the first time advertisers had stooped to using popular usage to make a point. Fifty years earlier, the sides of barns all over the country were plastered with endorsements for Red Man chewing tobacco by the great Philadelphia second baseman Nap Lajoie: "Lajoie chews Red Man, ask him if he don't." But no critic ever deigned to notice this sort of thing until the 50s, that golden age of American paranoia, when Madison Avenue vied with Moscow as the insidious corruptor of American mores. That was when the martini-sipping ad man in the gray flannel suit became the new archetype of the American smoothie — the character played by Tony Randall in *Will Success Spoil Rock Hunter?* and by Gig Young in just about everything else.

Maybe that's why the grammarians' criticisms of the advertisements echoed with charges of class treason, the sense that the Winston copywriters were probably Yalies who knew perfectly well when to use *as* and when to use *like*. As Jacques Barzun put it, "The language has less to fear from the crude vulgarism of the untaught than the blithe irresponsibility of the taught."

In retrospect, it's all pretty ironic. Those cigarette ads do indeed sound a little sinister to us now, and of course they came back to haunt the companies that produced them. But the worst thing critics could find to say about them at the time was not that they were selling cigarettes, but only that they were doing it ungrammatically.

The advertisers are still playing fast and loose with the language, but it's unlikely that the Winston episode will ever repeat itself. In recent months, for example, the Toyota people have been running a campaign that stresses how well their products fit in with consumers' day-to-day needs. "Toyota, everyday" is the slogan. You'd think that by spelling *everyday* like that they'd worry about suggesting that their products are banal and ordinary. But the ad agency thought the one-word version looked zippier, and when they talked to consumer focus groups, it turned out that no one was particularly troubled by the misspelling: people said they were used to seeing mistakes in advertising, and besides, it made the company seem folksier.

Indeed, folksy is all you see in advertising nowadays. You think of those in-flight infomercials where guys in jeans and Doc Martens are touting the latest cool stuff from Hewlett-Packard and Motorola. Not long ago, in fact, Microsoft went to the ad agency that had done all those Gen-X ads for Nike and asked for an ad series that would make them sound cool. It bothered some people, like the *Los Angeles Times* columnist Gary Chapman; he took to task all these multinationals who appropriate a style and language that originates with inner-city kids who will wind up being the losers in the information age. It was a perfect reversal of the attacks that critics leveled at the Winston people back in the 50s. The advertisers are still taxed for their linguistic condescension, but now their crime is the betrayal not of their own class but of the people whose language they're ripping off.

Well, of course. Advertisers are no less shameless now than they were back in the days of the singing commercial. What's surprising is only that people can still get indignant about it. Shocked, shocked! to find that there is advertising going on.

# Go Figure {1998}

There was a front-page article in the *New York Times* not long ago that talked about how the New York City police were not enforcing jaywalking laws, which was saving people a lot of tsoris. It was sort of funny to see that word there, particularly in a story that the *Times* ran in its national edition. You figure maybe they ought to have run a little footnote for their readers in Boise or Little Rock who aren't used to hearing Yiddish words bandied back and forth across the deli counter: "*Tsoris* (from Yiddish): Trouble or aggravation." But when I did a database search I found over four hundred press citations for the word over the past ten years or so, under any of six different spellings, and by no means all of the citations were from New York papers or were used in particularly Jewish contexts. For example, there was one story in the *Washington Post* that talked about all the tsoris that Queen Elizabeth has had with her family. That one brought me up short because I had a little trouble imagining the Queen herself using the word — "Oh, Philip, if you knew the tsoris I've had with my mishpokhe."

Then again, you never know. Yiddish words and expressions seem to be increasingly common these days, and it's not only Jews who are using them. Not long ago I heard an Irish-American real estate broker say, "Once they get finished paying the taxes, they won't be left with bupkes." I was impressed that he knew the word, though I doubt that he knew it originally had the literal meaning "goat turds."

It's true that American English has always been pretty open about borrowing words from other languages. But we tend to stop borrowing from a language once its use begins to wane, and the words it has already given us become thoroughly

Americanized. You look at all the words we borrowed from Dutch in the seventeenth and eighteenth centuries — words like *waffle, boss, stoop, poppycock,* and even *Yankee* — and nobody has any idea that they were once foreign, whereas the Yiddish words in English retain a foreign feel. In fact we seem to have a preference for borrowing the ones that sound particularly Yiddish, like *schlemiel, schmooze,* and *chutzpah.* What's more, their use seems to be spreading at a time when Yiddish itself has pretty much disappeared from view. It would be going too far to call Yiddish a dead language, but most younger American Jews now know only a couple of dozen words of it, and have no memory of the lively secular Yiddish culture that was so prominent in politics and the arts in the early years of the century.

Actually that may be connected to the reason why Yiddish words are on the upswing. It's as if something happened in the American imagination that transformed Jews from an ethnicity to a character type, the slightly self-deprecating, sardonic observer who gets to say things that Gentiles can't say about themselves. You think of Woody Allen in *Annie Hall* and of all the TV comedies that are more or less modeled on that movie, like *Anything but Love, Mad About You,* and even *Seinfeld.* It gives non-Jews a new license to use Yiddish words themselves, as if to signal their own ironic detachment from the passing scene. It's not that they want to think of themselves as Jews now, but that they like to think of themselves as shiksas and shegetzes.

Of course people don't always use the Yiddish words correctly. Take *shmuck.* In Yiddish it's a name for the penis which is also used to mean a stupid person, as in "What a shmuck I was not to buy Cisco at 20!" But nowadays I keep hearing people use it to mean something like "bastard," as in "He's a real shmuck to his employees." My theory is that when Gentiles hear *shmuck* used in such a vehemently disapproving way they think it must mean something stronger than merely a fool, not realizing that Yiddish culture considers stupidity to be one of the cardinal vices. As the linguist Ellen Prince has pointed out, Yiddish has more words for stupid or foolish people than the Eskimos are supposed to have for snow — *shmuck, shlemiel, shlemozzle, shmendrik, shmegeggy, shnook,* and *putz,* not to mention less well known items like *nar, flaterkop,* and *moyshek-apoyer,* which is a nice way of describing somebody who does everything backwards.

But I suppose this sort of reinterpretation is inevitable when these ethnic items are adapted for general consumption. And intermarriage does have its charms, whether it involves language, sex, or food. You walk into a bagel shop nowadays with a real sense of wonder. Who'd have thought you could take dense rings of boiled dough and cook them up into those agreeably fluffy concoctions stuffed with blueberries? Enjoy!

# The Past Is Another Country   {1998}

**I** was visiting friends in L.A. a couple of weekends ago. I wanted to go to the new Getty, but they said the lines would be too long. Instead they took me to the Autry Museum of Western Heritage, which opened a few years ago in Griffith Park. You'll be pleasantly surprised, they said, and they were right. There are some fine historical exhibits there, with appropriate multicultural nods to all the strains that came together in the old West—conquistadors, Comanches, cowboys, and the rest. It was only the name of the museum that gave me pause. Why "heritage"?

In fact *heritage* seems to have completely replaced *history* in the names of museums. There's an American Airpower Heritage Museum in Midland, Texas; a Motorcycle Heritage Museum in Westerville, Ohio; and an Anthracite Heritage Museum in Scranton, Pennsylvania. Not to mention a Jewish Heritage Museum in Atlanta, a Nordic Heritage Museum in Seattle, and heritage museums in other cities for Hungarians, Czechs, Irish-Americans, Native Americans, Italian-Americans, African-Americans, and women.

Actually this "heritage" business began in Britain, where the campaign to exploit historical monuments and stately homes spawned what the critic Robert Hewison has described as the Heritage Industry. Over the past few years, though, we Americans have been playing catch-up with a vengeance, and not just in the names of museums. Do a web search on *heritage* and you'll find sites for the McDonald's Heritage Bowl, Native American heritage collectibles, heritage glassware, heritage gift baskets, and of course the Heritage Foundation, that bastion of the American right.

The best take on the meaning of the word might come

from all the outfits that advertise what they call heritage furniture, including one that claims, "Many of our pieces are replicas of actual family heirlooms." "Replicas of actual family heirlooms" — that seems right on for the general sense of the word, though in the case of the museums you might want to change it to "replicas of actual families." At least when ethnic groups and nationalities talk about "heritage," they're looking at the past the way a family looks at its remote ancestors, as a source of distinguished portraits to line its walls. It's a relentlessly upbeat word, which leaves no place for the possibility that our ancestors were rapacious or stupid or just plain incomprehensible to us. There's no sense there that the past might be another country; it's just a long whiggish progression as the world got ready for us.

Maybe this is what "the end of history" should really mean. Either we mine history for the mantelpiece souvenirs that we can label as heritage or we flatten it into anonymous folklore. That's what has happened with the word *traditional*. It used to apply to things handed down orally with no known source or author — ballads, quilt designs, pumpkin pie recipes. But then about fifty years ago people started to apply the adjective to things like houses, furniture, and weddings. *Traditional* here doesn't actually have much to do with the older sense of the term; it's more just a way of evoking nostalgia for some imaginary idyll of American middle-class life, before modernity changed things for the worse. When people say they grew up in a traditional house, you can be sure they're not talking about the shacks or tenements that most of our ancestors actually lived in. Nor for that matter are they talking about a Southwest adobe dwelling, even though the roots of that style go pretty deep in American soil. Odds are they have in mind a tract house in Cape Cod or Tudor style that was thrown up by a developer some time in the 1920s or 30s and furnished in the pastiche of

New England and French provincial chairs and bedroom sets that stores call traditional furniture.

As it happens, it was just about the time that people started talking about traditional houses and furniture that they started talking about notions like traditional values and the traditional family. Those are just names for the way we imagine things were around the colonial-style dinner table of those traditional houses: a world where everything was clear and straightforward, with no moral problem so vexed you couldn't set it straight in a ten-minute heart-to-heart with Spencer Tracy or Lewis Stone. *Traditional* smoothes out the wrinkles of social history in exactly the same way it smoothes out the differences between styles of chair legs.

Of course, historians have always tailored their tales to the times, but I doubt that any age has ever been as efficient about the process as we are. Our predecessors merely rewrote history; we're doing away with it altogether. It makes you long for a time when people did their forgetting more, well, traditionally. As Marguerite Yourcenar said, we always rebuild monuments in our own way, but we ought to try to use the original stones.

# Yadda Yadda Doo   {1998}

I had a call from CNN asking me about the linguistic effects of the *Seinfeld* show. What kind of mark would it leave on the English language? Ten or twenty years from now, will we still be saying "Yadda yadda" and "Master of my domain"?

It isn't likely. TV shows almost never leave any permanent linguistic residue behind them. Of course just about every popular show has a phrase or two that work their way into general circulation for a while. Depending on when you came of age, your memories of the TV of the period are peppered with lines like "To the moon, Alice," or "Dy-no-mite," or "Isn't that special?" But when people say these lines it's almost always by way of alluding to the shows, and the phrases start to become outmoded once the show goes out of prime-time broadcasting. There are a couple of exceptions, like Sergeant Friday's "Just the facts," or maybe "Beam me up, Scotty." And I like to think I am doing my own small part to ensure that "Who loves you, baby?" will remain in circulation after all memory of *Kojak* has disappeared from the collective imagination. But most of the famous TV lines have a pretty short lifetime. When was the last time you heard anyone saying "You bet your bippy" or "Yabba dabba doo"?

Lines from movies are different: they're always detaching themselves and entering the language under their own steam. A lot of people use the line "We don't need no stinkin' badges," but not many of them could identify it as a quote, or actually a misquote, from *The Treasure of the Sierra Madre*. Ditto the Bette Davis line "What a dump!" from the 1949 film *Beyond the Forest*. Or how about "It seemed like a good idea at the time"? It originally came from the 1931 movie *The Last Flight*. And then there are all the famous lines which people can still identify but which they use without really invoking the movies they came from — "I could have been a contender"; "Make him an offer he can't refuse"; "What we have here is a failure to communicate"; "Go ahead, make my day."

Why are lines from TV so much more ephemeral than those from movies? One difference is that broadcast TV serials are collective experiences. We grow old with the shows and they grow old with us. And when hit shows die, at least in their network broadcast versions, we go through official mass interments like the one that's going on this week for *Seinfeld*. The shows may hang around for years in syndication, but it's only aficionados who go looking for them. Even when you run into an episode you've never seen, it just isn't compelling in the same way that it is on first-run broadcast, where everyone in the country is watching the same episode at the same time on Thursday night. It's like having lunch with an old lover — the language you used to speak seems quaint and stiff, even if you can still feel a nostalgic pang or two.

And what show was ever better suited to this fate than *Seinfeld*? That's how all the characters sound already. "Get out of town," "No soup for you" — the characters say those lines as if they're quoting them, trying on clichés like ties from a discount rack. When you come to think about it, in fact, the characters on *Seinfeld* talk exactly like the sorts of people who are always quoting old TV shows. You have the sense that these aren't people who spend a lot of time watching first-run shows like *ER*, or indeed any network program except *Melrose Place*. They're locked in front of reruns of *Man from U.N.C.L.E.* and *Superman*. And as you plow through all the coverage on the last episode of the show, it strikes you that that's how people have been talking about *Seinfeld* all along, with the obsessive attention to trivial detail that you usually associate only with Trekkies.

The fact is that *Seinfeld* has been a rerun since its first episode, with the archival smell that it took a classic like *I Love Lucy* a couple of generations to achieve. Not that there's anything wrong with that.

# Gen Z and Counting {1999}

**W**hat are we up to by now, Gen Z? It's September, and the registration lines at colleges are filling up with the new freshmen of the class of — are you ready for this? — 2003. By way of helping its faculty get their heads around that number, Beloit College has assembled its annual list of how the incoming students differ from their elders in their frame of reference. So far as the students born in 1981 are concerned, John Lennon and John Belushi have always been dead, the musical *Cats* has been on Broadway forever, and Yugoslavia never existed. And the students have replied with their own list of things they know about that their elders don't: Trapper Keepers, Tina Yothers, "Wax on, wax off."

Of course you could have made lists like this for any generation in the past. Still, there's one thing that does make the class of 2003 qualitatively different from earlier generations — these kids have never known what it was like to be young in an era when older people didn't hang on their every word. What brought this to mind was a piece in *The New Yorker* a few weeks ago about a pair of young marketing consultants who specialize in taking corporate clients on guided tours of the youth culture in New York's outer boroughs. They'll take a group of Ford executives from Detroit, say, and give them a quick immersion course. They warn them off wearing dock shoes and pink polo shirts and they teach them a little current slang — use *wack* to mean "bad" and *dope* to mean "good." Then they all go off to visit hip-hop stores and pass out free CDs to lure kids into stopping to talk about their language, their fashion, and, by the by, the brands they like. The tour has evidently become the latest hot ticket in the world of marketing.

The kids in the class of 2003 may find it surprising to know that there was a time when this would have been considered a pretty weird thing to do. For the last three hundred years, the natural course of getting older was that at a certain age you stopped using your own slang and started deploring the slang and habits of the next generation. Jonathan Swift condemned the slang of the young fops of his period as "barbarous mutilations." The Victorians liked to compare slang to a pestilence. Around 1850, Dickens' friend George Sala described it as "sewerage," and around the turn of the twentieth century another writer compared the fashions and slang of young people to "the mud and slime that is brought to the surface by the stir of the lower life ... from the saloon and the gutter." By the 1920s older people had begun to lighten up a little on youth and its language, but they were still pretty critical. H. L. Mencken ridiculed flapper slang and described the flapper as "a young and foolish girl, full of wild surmises and inclined to revolt against the precepts ... of her elders."

Thirty years later the culture of 50s rock 'n' roll evoked reactions that ranged from hysteria to comic ridicule. Frank Sinatra was quoted in the *San Francisco Examiner* as calling rock 'n' roll "the martial music of sideburned delinquents all over the earth." (I have my doubts as to whether he actually uttered those very words, but there's no question that he shared the sentiment.) Another critic deplored the tendency of white youth to adopt a slang full of "coarse Negro phrases." And on a lighter note, Steve Allen did a regular shtick on his weekly comedy show by giving poetic readings of the lyrics to rock 'n' roll songs like "Ramalamadingdong" (a song by the Edsels, by the way, whose name presumably had no endorsement from the Ford management of that period).

It's hard to pick the exact moment when all this invective started to wind down. Some people would point to the Beatles and Dylan, when the language, music, and culture of young people began to appeal to a general audience. Or maybe the turning point came a little earlier than that, in 1961, when Joey Dee and the Starlighters released "Peppermint Twist" and middle-aged New Yorkers began to line up outside the doors of the Peppermint Lounge. Or you could pick the year 1968, when *Hair* opened on Broadway.

It took a while for the tirades to die out, of course. In the 60s there were people denouncing the twist as a "jungle dance," and people said similar things about the dress and language of Woodstock. In the end, though, all these condemnations were bound to fade away under the benign tolerance of market capitalism. You can still find people who deplore the way kids dress and talk nowadays, but it's a safe bet they don't work for Ford or Nike or the Gap.

It leaves you feeling a little sorry for those kids lined up at the college registration desks. Whatever they wear, whatever they say, there's no one left to scandalize; there's no style they can come up with that the marketers can't repackage and sell back to them with an air pump in the tongue. There's nowhere to hide when Microsoft and Motorola are all over them hawking "cool stuff." Maybe that's why today's young people have been driven to tattoos, piercings, and general self-mutilation — emblems a little harder to co-opt than slang or clothing, though a little harder to throw aside when they get old.

# Wordplay in the Country {1999}

The best movie about country music I know of is a gritty little 1972 film called *Payday*. Rip Torn gives an intense performance as a fading, second-tier country star touring the South from roadhouse to roadhouse on an out-of-control, drunken binge. The movie is much more genuine than Robert Altman's overblown *Nashville*, which came out a few years later, and one reason is that it took pains to get the music right, both the best and the worst of it.

There's one scene in particular that sticks with me, when Torn's character is obliged to listen to a young country wannabe sing a composition called "I'm Loving You More and Enjoying It Less." It's the perfect example of an awful country song, right down to its title, a play on the slogan in a popular cigarette ad of the period. Pop singers like the Beatles and Elvis Costello may have visited wordplay from time to time, but country music lives there. A lot of it involves outright puns, like the Bellamy Brothers' "If I Said You Had a Beautiful Body Would You Hold It Against Me?" or Lee Ann Womack's "Am I the Only Thing That You've Done Wrong?" There's Gary Nicholson's "Behind Bars," which is about saloons, and Randy Travis's "On the Other Hand," which is about wedding rings. And then there are all those other titles that involve wordplay of one sort or another, like Dolly Parton's "It's All Wrong, but It's All Right," and Johnny Paycheck's "I'm the Only Hell My Mama Ever Raised."

When I think of songs like these, the singer who comes first to mind is George Jones. I don't know if he's done more of them than anybody else—the honors there probably go to Roger Miller or Johnny Paycheck. And a lot of the punning titles that Jones uses are just routine joke songs, like the recent "I Had

More Silver Bullets Last Night Than the Lone Ranger" or "She Took My Keys Away, and Now She Won't Drive Me to Drink." But Jones has also made a specialty of using puns and wordplay in the plaintive ballads that he sings like no one else — "A man can be a drunk sometimes but a drunk can't be a man," "At least I've learned to stand on my own two knees," or "With these hundred proof memories, you can't think and drive."

For some people, of course, this sort of punning just confirms a sense of country music as a linguistic trailer park. Since Tennyson's time, punning has been deprecated as the basest form of humor, to the point where it's often regarded as a kind of veiled aggressiveness. Habitual punsters live for groans the way violinists live for applause. Sophisticated people may make exceptions for the literary puns of Joyce or Nabokov or the urbane wordplay of 30s show tunes, but they have trouble finding a place for someone who makes puns in earnest, particularly in a sentimental ballad.

But maybe that's simply because most people have forgotten how to take puns seriously. The wordplay in Cole Porter or Nabokov is dazzling but usually superficial; the wordplay in country songs is pedestrian but sometimes profound. It has a rueful irony, as the innocent reading of an ordinary expression reveals a new meaning that makes it more sad and knowing. You think of Charlie Pride's "She's Too Good to Be True," or Jones's recent "Tied to a Stone."

It's a fitting device for these ballads, particularly when they're tackling their favorite theme — the fragility of happiness, love, and family. There's a joke that sums up the genre very nicely: "What do you get if you play a country song backwards?" — "You get your wife back, you get your dog back, you get your truck back..." And the sense of loss and estrangement is implicit in the language of the lyrics, too, as the ordinary expressions we use to talk about our lives break down to reveal darker meanings.

The wordplay has antique roots. It owes a lot to the language of sermons, particularly in the Baptist and Evangelical traditions, with their attentiveness to the multiple meanings of scriptural passages. But it has earlier antecedents in the sermons and poetry of the metaphysical poets, like Donne and Herbert. And even earlier than that, you can find its secular echoes in Shakespeare. Take Hamlet's bitter pun about his uncle, "a little more than kin, and less than kind." What a great title for a George Jones song.

# Turn-of-the-Century {2000}

**B**y the time February 2000 rolled around, people seemed to have stopped referring to the new millennium so much. That's just as well, since a thousand years is an absurd time span for a secular culture to bother about. But the change of centuries isn't proving so easy to get used to. Take the way we report dates. The other day I found myself saying that such-and-such a word was invented "back in the eighties." Then I stopped and changed it to "back in the nineteen-eighties." The phrase wasn't ambiguous, really, but the point of reference had changed. In a way it feels like the shift we have to make every Monday morning, when we go from saying "I saw him Wednesday" to "I saw him last Wednesday." We reach some arbitrary point on the calendar and we have to change the way we talk about the past.

For example, I keep hearing people start to talk about "the beginning of the century" and then stop themselves and say, "I mean, the beginning of the last century." But it feels a little odd to put things that way — and not just the way it feels odd to write "00" on our checks, which we all got over in a couple of weeks. The fact is that for all the brouhaha that led up to the millennial transition, we still think of our own period as beginning with Picasso and the Wright brothers and World War I, whereas Manet and Samuel Morse and the Civil War belonged to a different age. And it isn't as if anything happened on New Year's Eve that suddenly snipped that thread.

You get the same unsettled feeling when you think about how the future will refer to our period. There was a lot of talk in the press and over the Net last year about what we would call the first decade of the century — would it be the ohs, the double zeroes, the oughties, the naughts, or whatever? Frankly, it's hard for me to get very interested in this; I suppose we'll settle on one of these once the decade has been around long enough for people to make some generalizations about it. But what about another term that people will almost surely use to describe this period — the adjective *turn-of-the-century*? I can see why nobody got around to mentioning this one last December, when we were thinking of ourselves as poised on a peak between the ages, looking back on the thousand years that rose up to our feet. It's a little deflating to go from that grandiose height to being merely "turn-of-the-century." All of a sudden we're realizing that our successors are going to see us the way we see those folks in old-style hats and coats from the last time we went around, only we're a lot less dapper. We can live with knowing that future ages will find us ignorant — that's what gives us license to condescend to our own predecessors. But it grates to think they'll find us quaint.

But then, it isn't certain that people a hundred years from now will think of this moment at all, or that they'll think of it with the kind of auspiciousness that it has for us. After all, it hasn't been that long that people have thought of history as bundling itself neatly into centuries. If you were living in the year 1600 or 1700 you knew what the year was, of course, but you didn't necessarily feel you were living a moment of transition, the way you would if a dynasty fell. Even in Jane Austen's time most people didn't have that sense of dates as the signposts of human progress, or not in England, anyway. That's a point that struck me when I was watching the recent movie version of *Mansfield Park*, which has one character saying, "This *is* 1806, after all." That line wasn't in the novel; in fact it wasn't something that anyone in a Jane Austen novel would ever have uttered. But it wouldn't have been out of place in a novel by Trollope sixty years later. By then the perception of historical periods had changed — people saw them as shaped by universal forces that corresponded to the divisions of clock time, as the whole world marched forward arm in arm to the same regular measures. That was when museums started organizing their collections by century, and it was when people started using the name of the current century in the titles of book series or encyclopedias. This was a theme that people in the twentieth century enlarged on — the only century to stick its name on trains and movie companies. (Actually I started to say "the theme that we enlarged on," but I can't use that first-person plural pronoun to refer to the inhabitants of the twentieth century anymore, can I?)

The domain name *21stcentury.com* has been taken, but I don't know that it will have much of a market value fifty or a hundred years from now. The century is a pretty arbitrary chunk of time, and there's no reason to suppose that people will continue to attach any importance to the unit, or that they'll think of us as having any special relevance to them just because we happened to inhabit the world just after the odometer rolled over.

# word histories

# Hoosiers   {1989}

The great Hoosier hubbub began in March 1987, when Senator Alfonse D'Amato of New York predicted on the Senate floor that Syracuse, his alma mater, would beat the Indiana Hoosiers handily in the NCAA basketball finals the following day. He went on to make fun of the Indiana team, noting that Merriam-Webster's *Third International Dictionary* defined *hoosier* not only as "a native of Indiana" but also as an "an ignorant rustic."

But Bobby Knight's Hoosiers squeaked out the game by one point, thanks to Steve Alford's outside shooting. And the next day Indiana's junior senator, Dan Quayle, took the floor to congratulate the Indiana team and to propose that the Senate adopt a nonbinding resolution that would redefine the word *hoosier*: "Be it resolved that a Hoosier is someone who is smart, resourceful, skillful, a winner and brilliant."

All of this was just routine senatorial hijinks, but Quayle was apparently in earnest. According to a story that appeared in the *Washington Post*, he wrote to William Llewellyn, the president of the Merriam-Webster Company, and asked that the offending definition of *hoosier* be replaced by his own definition. Llewellyn explained that dictionaries are in the business of reporting the way words are actually used, but added that if Quayle could persuade the rest of America to take up the new use of the word, Merriam-Webster would be delighted to include it in the next edition. When last heard from, Quayle's office was promising to continue the battle and threatening to ban Webster's *Third* from its bookshelves.

As it happens, Midwesterners have been using *hoosier* as a pejorative since the nineteenth century. According to *St. Louis Post-Dispatch* columnist Elaine Viets, in Missouri a hoosier is "a low-life redneck," somebody you can recognize because, as she puts it, "they have a car on concrete blocks in their front yard and are likely to have shot their wife, who may also be their sister."

The best guess is that *hoosier* is derived from the British dialect word *hoozer*, meaning "big or large." As early as 1832, the word was used in America to refer to a large or burly person; from there it was a short step to meaning "a big rustic, a galoot." This is probably what led to its use to refer to Indianans. In the nineteenth century there was a disparaging nickname for the inhabitants of just about every state. Texans were called Beetheads, Alabamians were Lizards, Nebraskans were Bug-eaters, South Carolinians were Weasels, and Pennsylvanians were Leatherheads. If it's any consolation to Senator Quayle, in fact, he could point out to Ms. Viets that folks from Missouri used to be known by the endearing name of Pukes. Originally these names may have been applied by the inhabitants of neighboring states, but most of them were adopted by the natives in what appears to have been a spirit of contrary frontier humor.

Nowadays only a few of these nicknames survive, usually for the sports teams of state universities, like the Tarheels and the Buckeyes. But these aren't fighting words anymore. Apart from Hoosier, the only nicknames that still have any pejorative associations are Okies and Georgia Crackers. (Some people say that *cracker* is a shortened version of *corn-cracker*, and others that it's from an old slang word for liar. Both could be right; etymology is not destiny.) The rest of the nicknames seem to have fallen victim to fastidiousness or to chamber-of-commerce boosterism. When you're touting the superior educational levels of your labor force in an effort to win a supercollider for your state, you're probably not going to refer to them as Beetheads. Then too, the ease of mobility and homogenized culture of modern America have tended to smooth out all these regional identities. Shelby Foot notwithstanding, we've come quite a way since the days when Thomas Jefferson could refer to Virginia as "my country." You come to think there are no differences at all anymore: Buckeyes, Lizards, Weasels, Leatherheads, and all the rest of us, all in button-down shirts, eating frozen yogurt, watching *Entertainment Tonight*. Except that the Hoosiers still have an edge from the three-point line.

# Easy on the Zeal   {1992}

September 1792, if you will cast your mind back, was a
critical moment for the French Revolution. A bit before,
the King had been captured at the town of Varennes as he
was trying to flee the country. As the French debated his
fate, a Prussian army bent on restoring the monarch advanced on Paris. Prudent citizens began to hedge their bets.
The artful Talleyrand, who had earlier made a successful
transition from courtier to revolutionary, found it expedient
to depart for England on private business. The storm broke
on September 2, with the news that the French army had
been defeated at Verdun. With the encouragement or tacit
approval of the authorities, paramilitary groups broke into
the prisons and slaughtered over a thousand inmates, many
of them royalists or priests who had refused to sign an oath
of allegiance to the revolution.

The September Massacres, as they were called, horrified all
of Europe and embarrassed even the authorities who had incited or condoned them. A certain linguistic distancing was
needed. Danton called the executions "an unavoidable sacrifice." Minister of the Interior Roland admitted that there had
been some occasional "effervescences" and acknowledged that
some citizens had been "overzealous." But he went on to insist
that the majority of the victims were guilty of crimes and that
the authorities could not have foreseen or prevented the excesses. Nor should the enemies of the people be allowed to use
the affair to discredit honest citizens, he declared. This was too
much for Edmund Burke, that implacable opponent of the revolution, who excoriated Roland for his euphemisms: "When
[Roland] speaks to the populace . . . the whole compass of the

language is tried to find synonymies and circumlocutions for massacre and murder."

I'm not sure exactly what brought this episode to mind as I was reading about the controversy surrounding Darryl Gates, the Los Angeles chief of police. Maybe it was simply the coincidence that the L.A. affair began with the arrest of a fleeing suspect named King. But the rhetorical similarities were intriguing. Here was Chief Gates explaining the abuse of a prisoner in police custody as an aberration and an unfortunate excess. And here again were those references to a regrettable "over-zealousness," this time in the unlikely mouth of Bob Hope, who rallied to the support of his old friend Gates by saying that "just because a couple of officers were overzealous doesn't discredit the thousands of good ones."

I'll grant you that the analogy is only approximate, but it's curious that there should be any linguistic resemblance whatsoever. After all, most euphemisms live brief lives. Their cover becomes threadbare after a while as they mold themselves to the shape of the things they were supposed to conceal. *Liquidate, execute, terminate* — they all lost their euphemistic flavor after a few years. So *overzealous* has had a remarkably long run as an excuse for crimes and misdemeanors. You can find the word in contemporary accounts of every affair from Wounded Knee to Watergate, testifying to the enduring belief that there's a special dispensation for abuses committed out of devotion to a cause.

By historical standards, Chief Gates got off lightly. Roland had to flee the country, and committed suicide when he learned that his wife had been guillotined, though not before she got off the most memorable line of the whole affair: "Liberty, what crimes are committed in thy name!" Danton was guillotined a while later. As usual, Talleyrand had the last word. He returned to France in 1795 and served as foreign minister under the successive regimes of the Directory, the Consulate, and Napoleon's Empire. After Waterloo he represented Louis XVIII at the Congress of Vienna, and when the Bourbons were deposed once more in 1830, he served the new July Monarchy. His enemies called him unprincipled, but he preferred to think of it differently. Sainte-Beuve reports that someone once asked him the secret of his political longevity. "N'ayez pas de zèle," he answered. Or loosely, "Easy on the zeal."

# The Decline of Slang   {1992}

I saw a survey once that showed that a poll of British critics had ranked George V. Higgins among the five great-
est postwar American novelists. I don't know why Higgins is
a prophet with so much less honor here, but it may be that
Americans are no longer interested in the criminal demi-
monde that Higgins writes about. Nowadays we seem to
prefer the imported, genteel delinquency of P. D. James or
the officially sanctioned thuggery of international spies. It's
a change of taste that shows up in the language as well, in
the decline of slang.

Since Shakespeare's time, the English language and its literature have been enriched by the language of thieves, gypsies,
vagabonds, and their colleagues. Dictionaries and glossaries of
slang began to appear as early as the sixteenth century. I have
an 1811 edition of *Captain Grose's Dictionary of Buckish Slang
and Pickpocket Eloquence, As Revised by a Member of the Whip
Club, Assisted by Hell-fire Dick*. It lists such words as *curmudgeon, cocksure, crony, bully*, and *slang* itself, all of which eventually passed into the standard language.

A lot of this language was first made familiar to polite society in what the nineteenth century called Newgate novels,
named after the prison. These enormously popular romances
about rogues and highwaymen were sometimes so laced with
underworld slang that they required footnotes. (Thackeray par-
odied the genre in *Vanity Fair*: "Is that your snum? I'll gully
the dag and bimbole the clicky in a snuffkin.") A few Victorian
reformers made an effort to portray the underworld in something more like its sordid reality; Dickens wrote *Oliver Twist* as
a kind of corrective to the Newgate novel. But the genre re-

mained popular through the end of the century. Max Beerbohm poked fun at John Masefield's fascination with low lingo:

> A swear-word in a rustic slum
> A simple swear-word is to some,
> To Masefield something more.

The fascination is easy enough to understand. For the Victorians and their successors, the underworld was just what its name implied, a nether region as dark and as elaborately structured as Dante's. It was the repository of all the violent and erotic currents that respectable society could not acknowledge in itself, and it provided names for all the things that respectable people found literally unspeakable. To Victorian ears, slang evoked a far more salacious tingle than it does for us, and the contemporary denunciations of it were correspondingly choleric — in a literal way. In 1859, the critic G. F. Graham compared the spread of slang to the cholera epidemics that had swept London in the previous decade: "We may regard [slang] in the light of a pest to society . . . . Now, the language of everyday conversation is suffering from this infectious disease, and it becomes the duty of every Englishman who has a proper feeling for his language, to refrain from this evil himself, and to throw in its way every possible discouragement." The notion of slang as a pestilence persisted throughout the nineteenth century; in 1893 one writer could say that "slang is to a people's language what an epidemic disease is to their bodily constitution; just as catching and just as inevitable in its run."

It wasn't until the Jazz Age that Americans began to lighten up on slang. By the 30s, the gangster movie and the detective thriller had the voices of the yegg and the grifter echoing everywhere in the land. Sam Spade could be disdainful of the language: "The cheaper the crook, the gaudier the patter." But most Americans were titillated and took up the lingo enthusiastically. The fashion was satirized in Howard Hawks's *Bringing Up Baby*, when society girl Katharine Hepburn spouts gangster slang in order to convince a Connecticut constable that she is really an escaped con named Swinging Door Susie, until an exasperated Cary Grant says, "Don't listen. She's making all this up from motion pictures she's seen."

But the romance of the underworld and its slang died shortly after the war, along with the notion of respectable society itself. The professional criminals and lowlifes are still around, of course — the working-class safecrackers, con men, and car thieves that Higgins brings to life in his novels. But once the middle class cut loose, it no longer had to live vicariously through underworld language. It's true that a lot of slang still comes from the language of inner-city blacks, who have always been citizens of the underworld in the traditional American scheme of things. But most modern slang has come from the specialized lifestyles of the white middle class itself; slang is the language of hippies, surfers, hot-tubbers, yuppies, druggies, swingers, hackers, and the rest. They're people pretty much like anybody else. Slang doesn't hint at forbidden mysteries anymore.

# The Last Galoot   {1992}

**W**hen I was in my teens I had a clear picture of how it was going to be. She was going to look like Jean Arthur or Barbara Stanwyck, and at a certain point she was going to stamp her pretty little foot and look up at me and say, "You big galoot, can't you see I'm crazy about you?" Only I grew up too short and too late. My frame is not what you'd call galootish, and the word was all but extinct by the time I reached my majority anyway.

I'll miss it, and I'm kind of puzzled it's gone. It's true that sometimes a word has to be put out to pasture when it has outlived its usefulness. I have a certain nostalgia for *antimacassar*, *furbelow*, and *poop deck* on purely phonetic grounds, but I can see that it would have been impractical to keep them around. And other words are predestined to burn out after brief, meteoric careers. It's not surprising that you don't hear *groovy* and *bitchin'* anymore. Words like those are the Nancy Sinatras and Village People of the English lexicon. But *galoot* had been doing quiet, useful work for over a hundred years, and it isn't as if there was suddenly nothing more to apply it to. The woods are still full of galoots — Randy Quaid, Roger Clemens, and John Kenneth Galbraith, among others — only now we have to find something else to call them.

It isn't just slang words this happens to. Whatever became of *dudgeon*, meaning "indignation," as in the sentence "Durocher stomps back to the dugout in high dudgeon"? This one had been around since the mid-sixteenth century, and then it suddenly dropped out of sight, like someone who stepped out to buy a pack of cigarettes in August 1952 and was never heard from again. Yet you look around you and it seems as if the stock of indignation is as high as it ever was.

I have a theory about words like these. When you look up *galoot* and *dudgeon*, you find them marked with the haunting phrase "of obscure origin." Lexicographers like to speculate about their origins, of course, and you can always find some word in another language that sounds like the word you're interested in. Eric Partridge thought *galoot* might have come from the Dutch word *gelubt*, meaning "eunuch," but he had no evidence for the connection, and no account of why that word should turn up in another language meaning "a boorish fellow." Or why not from the French *gueulotte*, meaning "glutton"?— you can make up your own story here. And *dudgeon* might have come from an obsolete word that refers to a kind of wood used for the hilt of daggers, though there seems to be no connection in meaning, and anyway, that other *dudgeon* is of obscure origin too.

There are a surprising number of words that seem to come out of nowhere like this—*gimmick, hornswoggle, coax, mug.* Even the common word *boy* didn't appear until Chaucer's time—quite a while ago, but pretty late in the game to introduce a word for the young male of the species.

I think of these as Heathcliff words, dark strangers that turn up to claim a place in the household of English. Some of them are sent to sleep in the barn, like *galoot* and *hornswoggle*. Others, like *dudgeon*, plop themselves down brazenly at the dinner table. Yet there's always something a little different about them. And maybe it's foreordained that one day they should slip away just as mysteriously as they arrived.

# Über and Out    {1993}

**B**y now you've all heard that Superman was apparently killed off in the last issue of *Superman*. Of course he isn't likely to stay dead. It's a safe bet he'll be brought back with a new secret identity and a new costume — he should definitely lose the cape, which evokes a troubling resemblance to the late Elvis, another personality of ambiguous vital signs. And the last sentence of the comic book suggested he may have a new name too: "For this was the day that a superman died." *A* superman — I had the sense they were trying to give the name back to the language as a common noun. Only it's a little late for that.

The word *superman* began with Nietzsche, who used the German word *Übermensch* to describe a person who had shaken free of the cloying resentments of Christian morality. Some philosophers have translated this as "over-man" or "beyond-man." But *superman* wasn't a bad choice when George Bernard Shaw introduced the word in English in the title of his 1903 play *Man and Superman*. At that time the prefix *super–* was chiefly used to mean "over" or "beyond" in learned words like *superabundant, superstructure,* and *supernatural*. But the word *superman* had a bumpy future from there on, and it took the prefix along with it.

One of the villains in this story was Nietzsche's sister Elisabeth, whose strange story is recounted in a new book by Ben Macintyre called *Forgotten Fatherland.* Elisabeth was her brother's match in dementia, if not in genius. She married an unbalanced character named Bernhard Förster, a disciple of Wagner and a rabid anti-Semite. In 1886 the two of them led a band of settlers to the jungles of Paraguay to found a colony called New Germany, hoping that an Aryan utopia would flourish in isolation from the influences of decadence and cosmopolitanism — which was to say, the Jews. When the colony failed a few years later, Förster committed suicide and Elisabeth returned to Germany. After her brother went mad in 1891, she devoted herself to caring for him and nurturing the cult that had begun to grow up around his work. By judicious editing and sometimes by outright forgery, she recast him as the prophet of German nationalism and racialism. She was an early supporter of the Nazis, and when Hitler came to power he made a number of pilgrimages to Weimar to visit the shrine that Elisabeth had set up to the philosopher, whose concept of the superman was now being offered as the philosophical progenitor of the Nazis' master race.

Nietzsche would probably not have approved. He claimed he was really Polish, and he had a distaste for both German nationalism and the German physical type — "those faithful, blue, and empty German eyes," as he put it in *Beyond Good and Evil*. As for anti-Semitism, he thought it a sign of feeble character. But the superman was tarred with the Nazi brush, and when the comic-book character was introduced in 1938, it was as an American response to the Nazi type. Like the Nazi version, our Superman was an exceptional biological specimen, an uncritical patriot, and something of a moral simpleton. The resemblance didn't escape American leftist critics of the period, who even perceived an ominous connection between the *S* on Superman's chest and the *SS* tattooed on the arms of Hitler's storm troopers. Of course there were differences; our Superman had curly blue-black hair that suggested a Mediterranean or Semitic origin. And several years after he first appeared, it was explained that he'd acquired his magical powers when he escaped from his doomed home planet to come to a new world under a yellow sun, a classic American fable of immigrant success.

The end of World War II left the Nazi concept of the

superman thoroughly discredited, with the Man of Steel in sole possession of the field. And the popularity of the character led in turn to a new use of the prefix *super*– to refer to anything that was grander or bigger than its predecessors: we got *superstar, supersavers, Super Bowl,* and *Super Tuesday,* not to mention *supermarket* and the oddly contradictory *superette.* From there it was only a matter of time until the prefix detached itself and set up a life of its own as an adjective of gushing approval: "Oh, that was just super." But superlatives like these have a short half-life; if the NFL were starting out tomorrow I suspect they would call their championship game the Ultra Bowl, the Mega Bowl, or the Extreme Bowl. In the course of things, the comic-book hero came to seem ... well, comic, and not even the industrious irony of three Richard Lester movies could redeem him. Nietzsche would be relieved.

# The Burbs {1995}

**I**f you're looking for a trenchant history of the postwar American city, you could do worse than Barry Levinson's semi-autobiographical movie *Avalon*, about a boy growing up in the Baltimore area in the early 1950s. Near the beginning of the movie the boy watches as his salesman father is mugged and stabbed in a downtown neighborhood. Shortly after that we see the boy coming out of his family's row house to find his mother standing by a moving truck parked out front. "What does it mean, the suburbs?" he asks. She is puzzled: "What does it mean? It's just a nice place to live. It's got lawns and big trees."

For most Americans of that period, the word *suburbs* had a spanking new feel about it. It seemed to come into the American lexicon around the same time as *crabgrass, barbecue,* and *carpool.* As it happens, that's off by about seven hundred years. The word *suburb* actually goes back to the late Middle Ages, when it referred to the areas outside the city walls where people relegated a host of illicit and noxious activities — the tanneries and slaughterhouses, the gambling dens and bordellos. The phrase "suburb sinner" had a long life as a euphemism for prostitute. That's what Shakespeare was alluding to in *Julius Caesar* when he had Portia say to Brutus,

> . . . Dwell I but in the suburbs
> Of your good pleasure? If it be no more,
> Portia is Brutus' harlot, not his wife.

The suburbs didn't start to become respectable until around the turn of the nineteenth century, when upwardly mobile Londoners began to take houses in semi-rural districts just outside the city center. One of the first of the new suburbanites was

John Keats, the son of a London livery stable keeper. In 1817 Keats moved with his friend Leigh Hunt to a cottage in the then-suburban neighborhood of Hampstead, where they could go for long walks in the nearby countryside and return home to see the city spread out before them. To an aristocrat like Byron, the neighborhood seemed to symbolize all of the lower-middle-class vulgarity and pretension of Keats's and Hunt's poetry. He dubbed the two "the suburban school" and likened them to clerks who put on their best clothes for a Sunday stroll in the countryside.

For the next hundred fifty years or so, the word *suburban* was tinged with disdain for the smug and narrow-minded values that those neat little villas and detached houses seemed to embody. (When Ezra Pound finally got around late in life to disowning his virulent anti-Semitism, he described it as "that stupid, suburban prejudice," as if the worst thing you could hold against it was its vulgarity.) And the disdain was equally strong among the artists and intellectuals of postwar America, who regarded the new suburban tracts as expanses of complacency and bland uniformity. Lewis Mumford described the Long Island development of Levittown as "a treeless communal waste, inhabited by people of the same class, the same income, the same age group, witnessing the same television performances, eating the same tasteless pre-fabricated foods, from the same freezers, conforming in every outward and inward respect to the same common mold." It was a picture that was reinforced by movies like *The Man in the Gray Flannel Suit* and Martin Ritt's *No Down Payment*, and above all in "Little Boxes," an anti-suburban anthem that was a surprise hit in 1963 for Malvina Reynolds:

> Little boxes on the hillside, little boxes made of ticky-tacky,
> Little boxes, little boxes, little boxes, all the same . . .

And there's doctors and there's lawyers and business executives,
And they're all made out of ticky-tacky and they all look just
the same.

This was outrageously condescending, of course, and critics like
Reynolds and Mumford never said exactly what the people
in those houses were supposed to have done with their lives
instead — stayed in their walkups and become folksingers, I
suppose.

Now, though, the very word *suburb* seems to be receding
from the consciousness of the people who inhabit such a place.
Maybe you have to live on the West Coast to appreciate the effect fully. My friend Dana Cuff, who teaches in the architecture
department at UCLA, begins every course by asking the students, "How many of you grew up in the country?" Maybe two
hands go up. "How many grew up in the city?" Another two or
three hands. "How many grew up in the suburbs?" No hands at
all. "Look," she says to the kids who haven't responded, "did you
live in a detached home? Did it have a lawn, a garage? Did you
go shopping at a mall?" "Yeah, sure," they say. "Well then, what
would you call it?" And they answer, "Oh, well, you know, it
was just a town."

The fact is that young people in California localities like
Torrance or Pleasanton really have no consciousness of living in
suburbs, and it's getting more like that in other parts of the
country as well. One reason, I suppose, is that these places have
become so self-sufficient that they no longer identify themselves in relation to a city. They have their own industrial parks
and offices, their own shopping malls, their own arts centers,
universities, sports stadiums; if they think of the city at all, it's as
another mall a couple of freeway exits away. And in part the
change has to do with a certain loss of racial memory, in the

literal sense of the term — a forgetting of the urban flight that drove people to these places a few generations ago. It's as if they feel they have nothing to apologize for anymore.

Urban planners and theorists, too, have been trying to move away from the word *suburbs*: they prefer to talk about "edge cities," "the metropolitan fringe," or "new urbanism communities." The Harvard urbanist Peter Rowe talks about the American "middle landscape," an amorphous territory shaped by highways, detached houses, low-rise buildings, and shopping centers. Still, there's at least one group that hasn't forgotten the word *suburb*: the people who were left behind in the first flight from the cities a couple of generations ago. You still hear the word in rap songs, as in these lines from Ice Cube's album *AmeriKKKa's Most Wanted*, where he uses it to refer to the places where middle-class whites live:

> Word, yo, but who the fuck is heard?
> It's time you take a trip to the suburbs.
> Let 'em see a nigger invasion
> Point blank, on a Caucasian.
> Cock the hammer and crack a smile:
> "Take me to your house, pal."

It's ironic that *suburbs* would wind up being used this way, since in fact the neighborhoods that the gangsta rappers come from, like Compton and South-Central L.A., have detached houses and lawns and trees, just like the place the characters in *Avalon* moved to after the war. But for a lot of people the suburb has become a social category, not a geographical one. There's still a line between the 'hood and the burbs — but unlike Keats, we can't see it from a distance anymore.

# Rebirth of the Cool {1996}

When I heard last week that Gerry Mulligan had died, I had a sudden image of the grainy photograph of him on the cover of my first LP. The record was given to me when I was nine by a friend of my parents who found out that I was taking saxophone lessons. It was called *Konitz Meets Mulligan* and it featured the two saxophonists plus Chet Baker on trumpet and Joe Mondragon on bass. I haven't heard it for thirty years or more, but I can still scat for you all the solos in "Too Marvelous for Words." It was pretty amazing, not at all like "The Bluebells of Scotland," which we were rehearsing in the school band. The liner notes said that what they were playing was cool jazz. I'll say it was.

There were a lot of white kids back in the 50s who learned about cool from Gerry Mulligan, whether from his own playing or from the arrangements he did for other musicians, especially the epochal *Birth of the Cool* LP that Miles Davis recorded in 1950. It was at just about that time that the superlative use of *cool* surfaced in the mainstream press, though it had been around in black speech for at least twenty years before that. Jonathan Lighter's *Historical Dictionary of American Slang* gives a citation from *The New Yorker* in 1951, which felt the need to explain to its readers that cool was "the current word for hot in musical terminology."

The midwife of cool was the hipster, the type exemplified by Chandler Brossard, Lord Buckley, and Lenny Bruce, not to mention legions of wannabes who assiduously practiced snapping their fingers on the upbeat. That was the figure Norman Mailer described in his famous essay "The White Negro," which presented the hipster as an urban adventurer, a new phenomenon in American life. "[He] moves like a cat," Mailer said, "slow walk, quick reflexes; he dresses with a flick of chic." Above all, the hipster spoke a new language that "gave expression to abstract states of feeling," a process Mailer exemplified with the sentence "That cat is really on his groove, dad."

In retrospect, it's hard to believe anybody ever talked like that in earnest. That's the way slang is: outrageous on the way in, outlandish on the way out. And indeed, by all the laws of language, *cool* should have died a natural death around 1963 along with most of the rest of hipster lingo. It should have been replaced by *gear* and *fab*, which were themselves replaced by *groovy* and *far out*, which were replaced by *rad* and *boss*, which were replaced by *dope* and *hot*, around for a reprise. Who'd have figured that *cool* would survive the decade, much less the century?

Some people claim that *cool* has never been out of favor. As one friend of mine put it, Hey, *cool* is eternal. Others are sure the word fell out of fashion and was then revived. That's always the way it is with retro: it's hard to tell who just bought that furniture and who had it all along. The truth is a bit of both; over the last forty years or so, *cool* has undergone an almost constant series of revivals and redefinitions. The hippies picked up on it in the 70s and spun off a new antonym, *uncool*. A decade later, the surfers renewed it in the expression *way cool*. There's the rap *cool* of performers like Kool Moe Dee and Coolio. And finally there's the *cool* of the digital age — "Click here for cool stuff," or "Today's cool website." I call this one "terminal cool." Here the word has its own special pronunciation, a muffled grunt. *Coo-uhl. Coo-uhl.* Like pigeons under the eaves.

I suppose this is Mailer's vindication. Every time cool is reinvented, the hipster makes a flickering reappearance in American life — and never so immediately as now. It's of a piece with the revival of the goatee and the Gap ads that say "Neal Cassady wore khakis." And when you think about it, the hipster is a perfect model for the 90s — quietly disaffected, mordantly ironic, still working for Time Inc. and writing a novel on the side. In 1957 Mailer estimated that there were a hundred thousand hipsters in America; now you'd be hard put to find that many squares. Is everybody cool here? Solid.

# Remembering Ned Ludd    {1996}

**B**oethius wrote that every man dies two deaths: the first of his body, the second of his fame. Most of us count ourselves lucky if that second death is put off for a whole day, just long enough for our names to appear on the only page of the newspaper where the headlines are written in the past tense: WOLF J. FLYWHEEL, 82, WORKED IN LAW ENFORCEMENT. But occasionally fate makes a special deal with some people, which lets their names live on even after their fame has subsided. They don't have to give up their souls, just their capital letters, so they can continue as common nouns.

Take Charles C. Boycott, the nineteenth-century Irishman who was the first victim of a new kind of commercial embargo. Historians have no reason to remember his name, but etymologists are still keeping track of it. And then there's Charles Lynch, the Virginia magistrate known for administering a sort of rough-and-ready justice that came to be called lynch law. Or take my favorite of all, Frau Bertha Krupp von Bohlen und Halbach, who gave her name to the piece of artillery that was the original Big Bertha.

Sometimes a name comes down to us through a whole series of forgettings. Take Ned Ludd. The first bearer of the name was a fellow even less memorable than Boycott or Lynch. As the story goes, he was a feeble-minded workman who lived in a small town in Leicestershire near the end of the eighteenth century. It happened that one day he chased some boys who were tormenting him into a house where some frames used in stocking manufacture were kept. Unable to catch the boys, he vented his anger on the frames. Afterward, whenever machinery was broken it became the local joke to say that Ned Ludd had done it. The joke might have died out soon enough, but about thirty years later, when a band of Nottingham craftsmen took to breaking up machinery in a systematic way, their leader called himself General Ludd, and his followers became known as Luddites, a name that spread along with the movement to other parts of the English Midlands.

The modern myth holds that the Luddites were simply rioters who smashed machinery in the vain belief that they could somehow hold back the tide of industrialization, and since then people invoke the word whenever they want to suggest an irrational resistance to technological change. It has gotten to the point where you can't criticize any technological development without first abjuring any Luddite intentions. "Let me hastily assert that I am no Luddite," Robert Hughes assures the readers of *Time* magazine in the midst of a critique of the infobahn madness. "I'm no Luddite, but . . ." — it's the loyalty oath of the republic of progress.

The thing of it is that the Luddites were no Luddites either. It's true they destroyed machinery that enabled mill owners to replace them with women and children who worked sixteen-hour days for subsistence wages — this at a time when national unemployment was over thirty percent and relief for the poor was being drastically reduced. But what drove the Luddites to open rebellion was a series of legal measures that had stripped away their right to organize and eliminated the minimum wage, all in the name of free markets and the need to improve Britain's international competitiveness. And even then they were selective in their destruction: they spared the machines of mill owners who hadn't lowered their wages or who had compensated men put out of work.

The Luddites won some temporary local victories in places like Nottingham, where the minimum wage was restored. But in the end, with the full power of the state arrayed against it, the movement was doomed. Parliament made the destruction of machinery a capital crime, over the eloquent objections of Lord Byron. Twelve thousand troops were sent to the Midlands, more than Wellington had with him in the campaign against Napoleon. Some of the Luddites finished on the gallows, the rest went underground. Their story was rewritten as a lesson about the futility of trying to stand in the way of technological change. The victors have always written the history books, but in this case they wrote the dictionaries, too.

# Paparazzo and Friends {1997}

I rented *La Dolce Vita* the other night. That's something I do every year or two, but this time it was uncanny to watch, just a few weeks after Princess Diana's death. There's Paparazzo in a restaurant grabbing a photo of a prince with his mistress, Paparazzo in the back seat of Marcello Mastroianni's sports car urging him to go faster as they tail Anita Ekberg's limo, Paparazzo and a colleague jumping on a Vespa to chase Mastroianni and Ekberg as they leave a nightclub. You can see how the name would come to characterize the type. But it's a curious word for us to have. There is no shortage of English words formed from the names of fictional characters — *quixotic, narcissism, man Friday, Romeo, Mickey Mouse, Uncle Tom* — but *paparazzo* is the only one that comes from the name of a character in a foreign film. It makes the species sound like something recent and exotic, not a homegrown category. And that seemed to be an impression that British and American journalists were eager to foster in the wake of Diana's death. Listening to some of the British photographers, I had the sense they were relieved that the whole business had taken place on the Continent. "Oh, but that was in another country . . . ."

It's true that the paparazzo was a postwar phenomenon that first emerged in Italy. He was a creation not just of the liberated mood of the time but of technological innovations — lighter cameras, faster film, and the polychrome rotary press that had made possible the new photographic tabloids and magazines. (For that matter, I suppose he owed something to the motor scooter too.) All of this made possible new levels of intrusiveness. But there was nothing particularly new or foreign in the sensationalism of the popular press or the public hunger for juicy details about the lives of the famous.

What the critic Leo Braudy has labeled "the frenzy of renown" goes back to the eighteenth century. As far back as 1788 a British writer was complaining that newspapers "deal only in malice, or the prattle of the day." By the nineteenth century, the culture of celebrity was in full flower, and public figures had to be constantly on their guard. In 1865, when Charles Dickens was in a catastrophic train wreck in the company of his mistress, Nelly Ternan, his first thought was to climb out of a window to draw attention away from his traveling companion; when the first reporters arrived they found him heroically tending the injured at the other end of the train.

But it was here in America that the techniques of sensational journalism were brought to their modern perfection. By the end of the nineteenth century, mass-circulation newspapers were vying with one another in lurid accounts of grisly crimes and celebrity scandals, with a heavy pictorial content made possible by lithography. It was all aimed at capturing the attention of a readership that William Randolph Hearst described as "more fond of entertainment than . . . of information." The age came to be associated with another phrase which was based on the name of a fictional character and which owed a lot to technological innovation. In 1896 Joseph Pulitzer's *New York World* introduced the first regular comic strip in the form of "The Yellow Kid," whose hero was a brash gap-toothed slum kid who wore a bright yellow shift that was tinted by a new color process. The comic's popularity helped the *World* to become the first American paper to achieve a circulation of over a million, and other papers quickly got on the bandwagon. Their garish appearance led the journalist Edwin Warden to label them the yellow press. The comic pages soon went to full color, but *yellow journalism* stuck as a name for that freewheeling journalistic style.

At the time, the American press led the world in sex and scandal, but the British were quick to catch on with papers like Northcliffe's *Daily Mirror*, which was published in the new, smaller format that had been dubbed the tabloid when it was first introduced by the *New York World* in 1900. For half a century the press of the two nations ran neck and neck in lurid sensationalism. It was only around the time of World War II that the American yellow press began to fold or turn staid and suburban. On our side of the Atlantic that great stream of yellow ink was stanched to the trickle of the checkout-counter weeklies. Fortunately, though, the British papers weren't left to carry on alone. By then the Italians, French, and others had taken up the torch that was first lit in New York at the end of the last century. Hearst and Pulitzer would have recognized Paparazzo as their progeny.

# The Cult Quotient   {1997}

**N**ot long ago I gave expert testimony on behalf of a small religious group involved in a civil suit. They were submitting a motion to enjoin the other side from referring to them as a cult, on the grounds that the word was prejudicial and subjective.

It seemed a fair enough point to me. There are people who will tell you that cults are a well-defined category, but it'd be hard to show it from the way we use the word. There are a few certifiably deranged groups that everyone calls cults, like Heaven's Gate or the People's Temple, but beyond that it gets a little fuzzy. If you look on the web, you can find anti-cult sites that apply the word to everyone from Amway to Islam to the United Pentecostal Church. The press tends to be a bit more selective, but there's a lot of subjectivity there as well. In the interest of science I devised a way of calculating what I call a cult quotient, based on how frequently the press applies the word to a particular group. If you set the Presbyterians at 0 and Heaven's Gate at 100, then the Branch Davidians have a cult quotient of 96, the Scientologists are at 71, the Unification Church is at 62, the Transcendental Meditation people at 59, and so on down to the Jehovah's Witnesses at 21 and the Masons and Amway tied at 2.*

The fact is, the word is applied pretty arbitrarily. Take the Tibetan Buddhists. They have a cult quotient a lot lower than

---

*For the quantitatively minded, the cult quotient is computed as follows: Let $N_{1...K}$ be the number of occurrences of the names of varying religious groups in a newspaper database and $C_{1...K}$ be the number of occurrences of each of these names that fall within ten words in either direction of the words *cult* or *cults*. Let $R_i$ be the ratio of $C_i/N_i$, where $R_1 < R_2 < \cdots < R_K$. Then the cult quotient $Q_i$ for a particular name can be calculated as $100 \times (R_i/R_K)$.

the Sufis, the Hindus, or even the Mormons; in fact, they're on a level with the Methodists. But this means only that the Tibetan Buddhists are a politically respectable group whose American advocates are comfortably middle-class.

The one thing I learned that surprised me was how recent this pejorative sense of the word is. *Cult* didn't come into general usage until the nineteenth century, when it was just a slightly erudite label for a system of religious worship, particularly for ancient or exotic creeds like the cult of Aphrodite or the cult of Vishnu and the like. The word was also used metaphorically to talk about an exaggerated devotion to some idea or artist, like the Wordsworth cult. It wasn't until recent times that *cult* acquired a sense of spuriousness and social deviance. The earliest dictionary I found that includes that sense was published in 1961.

It's odd that we never had a special word with this meaning before then. After all, the history of American religious life is nothing but the account of one eccentric sect after another, from the Puritans to the Methodists to the Mormons to the charismatic and evangelical movements of more recent eras. And that's not to mention all those European secessions and schisms that fled to our shores so they could do their theological bickering undisturbed.

It's true that most of these groups were nowhere near so weird as Heaven's Gate or the Jonestown Temple. But they clearly struck contemporaries as being just as outlandish as the majority of the groups we call cults now. The nineteenth-century mainstream press heaped just as much ridicule on Joseph Smith and Mary Baker Eddy as its modern successors have heaped on L. Ron Hubbard and Sun Young Moon.

Where did this new idea of cults come from? In a word, from the East, along with the Eastern language and religious doctrines that began to have an influence in the West around the middle of the nineteenth century. Charles Dickens and Wilkie Collins were among the first to exploit this theme, with their fanciful tales of opium-smoking devotees of the Indian cult of Thuggee that the British had repressed in the 1830s. That connection gave us the word *thug*, not to mention a line of Orientalist melodrama that stretches directly down to films like *Help!* and *Indiana Jones and the Temple of Doom*. And there was all the muddled mysticism of the Theosophists and the spiritualists and their ilk — people like Aleister Crowley and Madame Blavatsky, who wrote about various Eastern cults and helped to popularize the word. (Madame B. also bears the responsibility for popularizing the word *guru* in the West.)

By the mid-twentieth century it seemed natural enough to extend the word *cult* to any small religious group that struck people as flaky, wherever it happened to originate. It may be that the shift of *cult* was helped along by an association with the word *occult*. There's no etymological connection between the two, but people tend to believe that cults have access to mysterious methods of mind control, whether in the form of some antique Eastern sorcery or the modern phenomenon of brainwashing. (That word was another Orientalist contribution to the concept of the cult, by the way. It was introduced during the Korean War to describe the Chinese method of indoctrination used on American POWs, offered as a literal translation of the Chinese expression *xi nao*, or thought reform.) It made for a reassuring account of where all those weird new religions were coming from. When you call them cults, they seem qualitatively different from the old-style religious zealots who were native to our soil.

# Portmanteau Words {1999}

In 1811 Governor Elbridge Gerry of Massachusetts enacted a redistricting of the state that was highly favorable to the Federalist Party. One of the districts was so oddly shaped that the painter Gilbert Stuart remarked to a newspaper editor friend that it looked like a salamander, and drew a head and claws on the map to bring out the resemblance. "More like a gerrymander," said the editor, who published the picture in the next edition of his newspaper.

That was the origin of the word *gerrymander*, which had the distinction of being the first portmanteau word coined in America — a word that's formed by blending together the parts of two other words. Actually it wasn't for another sixty years that the term *portmanteau word* itself would appear. We owe it to none other than Lewis Carroll, who based the notion on a large leather suitcase with two compartments. The term comes up in *Through the Looking-Glass*, just after Humpty Dumpty has recited "Jabberwocky," when he's explaining to Alice how he formed the word *slithy* out of *lithe* and *slimy*. "It's like a portmanteau," he says; "there are two meanings packed up into one word."

At the time Carroll was writing, though, there were only a few portmanteau words in English. *Dumfound* was one, formed from *dumb* plus *confound*, and so was *twirl*, formed from *twist* and *swirl*. But until modern times this was a decidedly minor way of making new words.

The vogue for portmanteaux really began around the turn of the twentieth century, with input from several disparate sources. The Soviets made this a favorite way of forming the names of organizations and policies, like *Comintern* from *Communist International*, and *agitprop* from *agitation* and *propaganda*.

The resolutely anticommunist *Time* magazine was no less creative, coining words like *cinemogul*, and so was the columnist Walter Winchell, who coined *infanticipating* for "expecting a child." These examples didn't really catch on; corporate America was more successful with product names, like *Peptomint* and *Dictaphone*. And journalists and publicists had a field day coining portmanteaux like *smog* from *smoke* plus *fog*, *motel* from *motor hotel*, and *brunch* from *breakfast* plus *lunch*.

The process picked up more steam after World War II, and it's been at full throttle in recent years. The entertainment people have given us *Cineplex*, *blaxploitation*, *infotainment*, *dramedy*, and *rockumentary*. Politicians have given us *Medicare* and *Reaganomics*. Businesspeople talk about *permatemps*, *infopreneurs*, *coopetition*. Technology's full of these too: *simulcast*, *netiquette*, *cybernaut*, and all the other terms popular among the people whom we call the *digerati*. There's no escaping these words even in daily life: "Hey, after we finish our dancercise, why don't we slip out of our tankinis and go out for a Frappuccino?" "Fantabulous!" In the past few generations, English has introduced more portmanteau words than in all the previous centuries going back to Chaucer. And this doesn't take into consideration all of the portmanteau corporate names that seem to make up half the stocks on the tech indexes: Microsoft, Trinitech, Unisys, Metricom, Infoseek, Logitech. There are naming consultants who have programs that can grind out endless lists of these things.

Why have people given us this pullulation of portmanteaux? In the words of the old punchline, because they can. Since the time of Elbridge Gerry, most successful portmanteau words have been coined by newspapers, press agents, government agencies, and corporations — people with the power to broadcast their coinings via the full apparatus of modern publicity. What better way to signal your influence than by putting a stamp on the language itself?

This helps to explain why portmanteau words are usually so transparent. In this sense they're the opposite of slang, which percolates into the language from cliques and in-groups and is usually designed to be opaque to people who aren't in the know. When you hear some Gen-Y person saying, "Wow, that's wack," you have no idea whether the word means good, bad, or expensive. But *dancercise, simulcast, Frappuccino*—they wear their meanings on their shortened sleeves. Portmanteau words are the sound bites of modern English, calculated to catch on the first time people hear them. I'm not sure if that Massachusetts newspaper editor would have gone ahead with *gerrymander* if he could have foreseen the day when *shagadelic* would be looking down on us from every billboard.

# Ten Suffixes That Changed the World  {1999}

You could recount a lot of the history of the century just by tracing the suffixes that have been in vogue from one decade to the next. Think of the territory that *–in* has covered, for example, in its progression from the drive-in restaurants and movies of the early 1920s to the sit-ins of the civil rights movement, the be-ins and love-ins of the hippies, and the teach-ins of the antiwar movement. The 40s had *endsville* and *splitsville* and *palookaville*, the 50s and 60s had *beatnik, neatnik*, and *draftnik*. There's the *–gate* of *travelgate* and *Monicagate* and the *–ercise* of *dancercise, jazzercise*, and all the other 80s and 90s fitness crazes. There's *.com*.

And then there's *–athon*. I was thinking about this one the other day when they held the walkathon at my daughter's school. Sophie did seventeen laps, and all her sponsors duly received notice of how much they owed toward the purchase of new playground equipment. It's a common ritual these days; the suffix *–athon* is having a monster decade. We have walkathons, bowlathons, swimathons, bikeathons, and danceathons. Christian radio stations have praiseathons, and the library of the University of North Texas recently held a barcode-athon to convert its books to an automated cataloging system.

I would have figured that *walkathon* and the others were pretty recent inventions, but in fact the *–athon* business goes back quite a while. It all started with *marathon*, of course, which entered English in 1896, when the first modern Olympic games were held. Marathon was originally the name of a place twenty-six miles from Athens where a famous battle was fought. (*Marathon* comes from the Greek word for fennel — a useful tidbit to have handy when conversation flags.)

But nobody thought of stripping the *—athon* off the end of *marathon* until the 1920s, an age obsessed with watching people do things for abnormal lengths of time. The public flocked to six-day bicycle races and made a hero of Alvin "Shipwreck" Kelly, who set a record in 1929 by sitting atop a flagpole in Atlantic City for forty-nine days. Then there were the dance marathons, which people started to call danceathons for short. Most of us remember these now from the 1969 movie *They Shoot Horses, Don't They?* Couples would dance for days or weeks on end for small cash prizes, with dancers occasionally collapsing or dropping dead on the dance floor. Some states tried to discourage these ordeals by passing laws that prohibited dancing for more than eight hours straight, and to get around these restrictions, promoters started holding competitions where dancers were allowed to walk around for brief rest periods. They billed these contests as walkathons, since there was no legislative time limit on walking contests.

Those early danceathons and walkathons were simply spectacles or publicity stunts; the connection between the suffix and charity had to await the introduction of television. Broadcast TV was still looking for its voice back in 1949 when NBC had the idea of holding the first telethon on behalf of the Damon Runyon Cancer Fund. The host was Milton Berle, TV's first big star. He remained on stage uninterruptedly for sixteen hours, apart from brief visits to his dressing room to shave and change his shirt. A stageful of models and showgirls handled the phones, with plainer operators taking calls backstage.

One of Uncle Miltie's guests on that occasion was a young comedian named Jerry Lewis, who seventeen years later would bring the telethon to its highest form of expression with the insight that the host must *not* shave or change his shirt. Over the course of the Labor Day weekend the entire country could watch Jerry grow increasingly rumpled and haggard as he draped himself around a series of winsome kids on crutches (a tableau that enriched the English language with the term *poster child*). The whole production was a clear improvement over the danceathons of the 20s: it gratified the same morbid voyeurism, but now you came away from it feeling edified.

The telethon gave rise to a clutch of charitable events like pledgeathons and callathons, though nothing has ever surpassed the Jerry Lewis telethons for sheer bathetic spectacle. But starting in the 80s, *–athon* took another turn, which united both its earlier senses — of sustained physical activity on the one hand and charitable giving on the other. Where young people used to raise money for a good cause by holding bake sales or car washes, now they get friends and relatives to pledge money in return for their performing some strenuous exercise to the point of near collapse. People from the 20s or 50s might have had trouble understanding what the one has to do with the other. But it's a natural fit for an age that thinks of running ten kilometers as a form of spiritual exercise — and all the more so if it's dedicated to a worthy cause. That's why even well-established road races and competitions have come on board by consecrating themselves to popular diseases.

There's something about all these modern walkathons and bikeathons that recalls the early Middle Ages, when you could acquire indulgences by paying other people to say masses or make pilgrimages on your behalf. The practice was finally discontinued when the church decided it rested on dubious theological grounds. But why? It seems a perfect system for everybody — or at least that's how it felt when the San Francisco School walkathon was over. The school raised a little money, the kids were glowing with righteous exhaustion, and we sponsors had the moral satisfaction of knowing that our donations were purely disinterested. After all, our cars were still dirty.

# The Edge   {2000}

I got an email from a friend of mine who was very excited about this guy she'd started seeing — "He has a great sense of sarcasm," she said. I was a little taken aback by that recommendation; I wrote her and said, "Gee, if I were the guy I'd have waited till later in the relationship to let on to that." But I was obviously thinking in terms of the old-economy sarcasm. For a lot of people now, *sarcasm* is simply a cover term for pointed humor of any kind, from satire and parody to simple banter. Go to the web, for example, and you'll find things like the Tolkien Sarcasm Site, which turns out to be just a collection of gentle gibes and spoofs. There's not much trace left of the original meaning of a word that's derived from the Greek for "tear the flesh."

What I took my friend to be saying was that the guy had what I would have called a good sense of irony. The distinction used to be clear, at least in principle. Both sarcasm and irony involve saying the opposite of what you mean. But with irony you're winking at your listener, whereas with sarcasm you're sticking out your tongue. Irony is a private joke, sarcasm is public ridicule.

Why did the boundary start to blur? At one point I thought it had to do with the fact that people have gotten a little unclear on the other meaning of *ironic*, where it points at how fate can frustrate our expectations. Nowadays, though, people often use the word with no sense of piquancy or ruefulness — it's just a synonym for *coincidental*. I hear sports announcers doing this all the time: "Ironically, he was wearing borrowed shoes the last time he kicked a fifty-yarder."

But it turns out that people have been using *ironic* in this loose way for more than a hundred years, and up to now it hasn't dislodged the other uses of the word or generated any confusion with *sarcastic*. And on reflection I don't think my friend was confused about this either — if the word *sarcasm* is replacing *irony* in her mind, it's because that's what's going on out there. Wherever you look, irony's moving out and sarcasm's moving in. Johnny Carson was ironic, David Letterman is sarcastic. *Peanuts* was ironic, *South Park* is sarcastic. Andy Warhol was ironic, Jeff Koons is sarcastic. John Waters is ironic, Todd Solondz is sarcastic.

The novel *Emma* was ironic and the movie *Clueless* was sarcastic — if you were making up a banner for the new sarcasm you'd write AS IF on one side and WHATEVER on the other. And most of the other recent Jane Austen movies allowed themselves a lot more sarcasm than the novels ever did. The extreme example was Patricia Rozema's *Mansfield Park*, which turned the novel's priggish heroine into a version of Jane Austen herself, only prettier and bristling with sassy retorts. It was something of a revelation for those of us who'd never thought of pairing Jane Austen with the adjective *in-your-face*. You had the sense that all she would have needed was a makeover and a couple of sessions with a personal trainer to take her place as a regular character on *Ally McBeal*.

But that's what has happened: sarcasm has gotten winsome, irony has gotten tired. There isn't much point to being ironic anymore, in an age that puts such a premium on knowingness. When Jane Austen was writing she could pretend that there were only about ninety-five people out there who were going to notice the irony; now everybody's taken a course in it. When you pick up a copy of Congreve or Fielding at a used bookstore, you keep running into these passages marked with yellow highlighter where students have written "irony" in the margins. But how are you going to sustain the tone of ironic innocence when there's nobody out there who isn't in on the gag?

The same loss of innocence that did irony in made it inevitable that sarcasm would be decriminalized. All in all, it's probably a healthy sign — it signals the disappearance of the constraints and inhibitions that irony festered in. Irony was always the recourse of people who weren't allowed to say what they meant. But who needs to be oblique or indirect in an age when *The New Yorker* is publishing four-letter words? Or just imagine somebody trying to be ironic on *Jerry Springer* — I mean, how would you tell?

For those of us who were raised under the old dispensation, of course, this decriminalization of sarcasm can take a while to get used to. We hear younger people saying things like "Duh" and "In your dreams" and we tend to read some malicious intent. But we ought to feel glad that they've been unburdened of that oppressive need to veil their aggressiveness. And they mean it in the nicest way.

# No Picnic {2000}

Not long ago a Stanford colleague forwarded me a posting that his niece had run into on an African-American Internet discussion list. It urged people to stop using the word *picnic*, which it claimed was derived from the phrase "pick a nigger." The story was that white people used to do lynchings as family affairs, where they would take a lunch along and play music, then pick a black person to hang from a tree. The writer went on to suggest that African-Americans would do better to use a word like *outing* or *barbecue*.

My colleague's niece had asked him if there was any truth to the message, and he forwarded it to me in my capacity as the local repository of curious wordlore. I wrote back to tell him that the etymology was bogus — in fact *picnic* goes back to a French word for a potluck dinner that was coined in the seventeenth century, a couple of hundred years before lynching became an American custom. My friend sent my message to his niece, who in turn forwarded the information to the list where she had read the original posting. But I don't have any illusions that this will do much to discredit the story. That *picnic* etymology has been circulating on the Internet for years, despite the numerous rebuttals that have been posted. The tale even surfaced in the press several months ago when African-American students at the State University of New York at Albany objected to calling a student-run event a picnic — a story that conservative columnists naturally were quick to pick up as their PC excess of the week. But that doesn't seem to have slowed it down either.

That's typical of the way these tall tales go round in cyberspace, always a step ahead of the law. But I have the sense that in this case these rebuttals miss the point. Of course the *picnic* etymology is silly — and unlike most urban legends, this one can be checked out just by opening a dictionary. But it isn't factual plausibility that makes for successful legends, urban or otherwise; what matters is their dramatic plausibility, which the picnic story has got down perfectly. It's a familiar theme in these tales, where inoffensive texts or images are always turning out to conceal some sinister sign. There are the dust clouds in *The Lion King* that are said to form the letters *S-E-X*, the Snapple label that contains a picture of a slave ship and an emblem of the Ku Klux Klan, the anti-Islamic message that appears in Arabic letters when you turn the Coca-Cola logo upside down. And what could be a better example than the story that a word as innocent-sounding as *picnic* conceals the first syllable of the ugly word *nigger*, as if to suggest that even the most wholesome institutions of American life are tainted by our history of racism?

This paranoid style is common in urban legends about race, whatever their point of view. But it's particularly compelling when you give the story a linguistic form — as if the word had a secret original meaning hidden in its syllables, like a virus in an email attachment. It's an idea that's in the background whenever people are concerned with the occult powers of words. And it isn't surprising that it should come up now in connection with the language we use to talk about race and gender, which is just the most recent episode in our age-old obsession with the way words can magically alter experience.

That's why the rebuttals to the *picnic* etymology seem beside the point; in the end these are really stories about syllables, not origins. Not long after I had the exchange with my colleague about the picnic story, he mentioned to me that he had a professor who always tried to avoid using the word *denigrate*, since it comes by its meaning via a Latin root that means "to blacken." I asked him if he thought his professor would have had the same feeling about *atrocious*, which comes from the Greek word for black. He got the point right away. "No," he said, "I guess it's just that *denigrate* has that syllable *nig* in it."

That kind of sound contamination is what led the mayor of Washington, D.C., Anthony Williams, to fire a white aide last year when he used the word *niggardly* in a discussion of the city budget. The press had a high time ridiculing the mayor on that one, pointing out that *niggardly* is an innocent word of Scandinavian origin which has nothing to do with the racial epithet. Still, it's a little disingenuous to pretend that you can pronounce a word like *niggardly* now without evoking the echoes of its homonyms. Phonetics always trumps etymology. We all learned that when we were six, as we discovered what scatological pleasure there could be in pronouncing an innocent word like *shampoo*.

# Community Sting {2000}

The title of Robert Putnam's recent book *Bowling Alone* is a reference to a curious trend in American life: while more Americans than ever are going bowling, there has been a precipitous decline in bowling leagues over the same period. For Putnam, the tendency exemplifies a much broader decline in participation in American civic life. PTA membership is down in recent decades, and so is membership in the Elks, Kiwanis, B'nai Brith, and the NAACP. Americans play cards less often than they used to, go to church less, and are less likely to get involved in political campaigns. All of these are signs of what Putnam describes dramatically as "the collapse of American community."

But if it's true that Americans have less of a sense of community than they used to, it certainly hasn't stopped them from using the word *community* more widely than ever before. Of course the word has been used for several centuries to refer to groups whose members are drawn together by some common circumstance that sets them off from the people they live among — the merchant community, say, or the British community in Naples. Nineteenth-century English Jews referred to themselves simply as "the community," in pretty much the same way that gays and lesbians use the phrase today. But alongside of these more-or-less traditional uses of the word, you find it applied to just about any group of people who share some property or interest, however incidental it may seem. Do a search and you'll find references to the rottweiler community, the Windows community, the vegetarian and vegan community, and the video-arcade-gamecollecting community. I ran into a regional transportation plan that talked about accommodating the needs of the pedestrian community (a group I commune with myself from time to time when my car is in the shop). And this is not to mention the left-handed community, the asthma community, the bail-bond community, the piercing and tattoo community, and the diaper community, which in case you're curious is a branch of the infantilist community.

Then there's just "the community," in the abstract, which is the term we apply to society when we want to paint it in a warm and deserving light. Expressions like "community service," "community relations," "give back to the community"— all of them have the positive connotations that are a defining trait of the word, however it's used. Whatever else it may be, community is good for you. Nations, states, classes, regions— those are all things that can sometimes make us nervous when they exert too strong a hold on people's allegiance. But nobody ever complains about an excess of community feeling. And just to ensure that community remains an absolute good, we withhold the word for any group that we disapprove of; people don't talk about the terrorist community or the Holocaust-denier community. It isn't that the members of those groups don't have common interests or convivial interactions, but for us the groups aren't bathed in the glow of positive sociability that the word *community* evokes. But of course this all depends on your point of view: the phrase "pedophile community" sounds pretty strange to me, but it turns out that pedophiles use it all the time.

The explosive growth of *community* began long before the Internet age. It got its first modern boost from the sociologists who popularized the word in the 1920s and 30s as a translation of the German *Gemeinde*, at a time when the American public was first becoming fascinated with social science. Among other things, that was what led home builders to begin using the word to describe the developments they were putting up all over the country. It enjoyed a further boom in the 80s with the rise of an identity politics that defined us all by our differences.

But it's only with the Internet that the word has achieved its current promiscuous versatility, as it becomes possible to organize a national conversation around any common interest or concern, however diffuse it may be. And like the housing developers of the 40s and 50s, web developers and others have been quick to perceive a commercial opportunity in the new uses of the word. Software companies offer "tools for building high-traffic community" around a website or a new video game, and most commercial sites have what's called a community page, where people can gather to commune about Campbell's soup or *Buffy the Vampire Slayer*. And software makers are in hot competition right now to develop "community portals" that are specialized to the needs of everyone in the Farmer's Insurance community or the purchasing-agent community.

If there's a silver lining, it's that the word is becoming so devalued that people may start to bail out on it. There's something about *community* that ought to make us nervous. It isn't just the rosy light it casts on whatever it touches but the one-size-fits-all elasticity that the word has acquired, which tends to obscure the loss of real community in American life. Community is on its way to becoming just another commodified American virtue, like heritage — you can buy it by the yard.

politics of the English language

# Force and Violence   {1990}

It's a cardinal rule of lexicography that you should avoid circular definitions. If you define the word *bobcat* as "a lynx," you had better make sure you haven't defined the word *lynx* as "a bobcat." But circularity isn't always easy to avoid. For example, Merriam-Webster's *Ninth Collegiate* gives one of the definitions of *force* as "violence, compulsion, or constraint exerted upon or against a person or thing." But then they use the word *force* in their definition of *violence*: "exertion of physical force so as to injure or abuse." It's a minor blunder, but it raises an interesting point. The dictionary may think that *violence* and *force* are alike in meaning, but unlike *lynx* and *bobcat*, they're not words you can use interchangeably.

Take the statement made by President Bush when he sent over four thousand troops to Los Angeles a couple of weeks ago: "Let me assure you, I will use whatever force is necessary to restore order. I guarantee you, this violence will end." It's clear what moved Bush to make that distinction. Force is the prerogative of official power; violence is the desperate expedient of the powerless. It isn't just a question of justification or legitimacy; we use the word *force* even when power is abused. Saddam Hussein tried to take Kuwait by force. The cops who beat Rodney King were charged with excessive use of force, but it was called violence when rioters pulled a driver from his truck and beat him. The videotapes of the two incidents may have looked eerily alike, but in the first case the perpetrators were wearing uniforms.

To check this theory about the distinction, I pulled five hundred citations of the word *violence* from a newspaper database. In all, the word was used only four times to refer to the actions of official authorities: twice for the Haitian army, once for the South African police, once for the former military regime in Brazil. The rest of the time, *violence* referred to unauthorized actions by soccer fans, rioters, strikers, gangs, demonstrators, guerrillas, and the like. Or often the perpetrators of violence weren't mentioned at all. It's striking how often the word *violence* is used as the subject of a sentence: "Political violence flared anew in Haiti," "A wave of violence has swept over this Central American country," "As violence rocked Los Angeles this week...." Violence breaks out, erupts, explodes, escalates, ebbs. We talk about it as if it were a thing with a life of its own, a kind of eczema on the social order; the people who do it are anonymous or irrelevant, like the passive hosts of a disease. Force, on the other hand, doesn't erupt by itself. It's always the object of the verb: someone uses force, deploys force, exercises force. You can see the difference in Bush's statement: "I will use whatever force is necessary.... I guarantee you, this violence will end."

But of course the violent acts of the powerless can be deliberate, premeditated, purposeful. And the Lord knows that the violent acts of official authorities can be spontaneous. If you wanted to describe accurately what we saw in the Rodney King video you might say that "force broke out," except that the English language doesn't allow us to put it that way. But the difference is only perspectival. If we speak of violence as a kind of autonomous condition, it's because the powerless are usually invisible until they act, whereas force comes from people we already have our eye on.

Indo-European had two words for fire. One denoted fire as an active, animate force; it's the root that shows up in our words *ignite* and *igneous*. (It's also the source of the Sanskrit name of the Hindu god of fire, Agni.) The other gave us *fire* and the prefix *pyro–*, the first from Germanic, the second via Greek. This was the word the Indo-Europeans used to talk about fire as a domesticated tool that could be put to doing useful work. But they must have realized that it was the same stuff and that it could burn you one way or the other.

# Eastern Questions {1991}

**P**eople often credit Hegel with having been the first to say that history repeats itself. But Montaigne made the same observation, and so did Plutarch, and so did Thucydides. One thing is sure: it was Marx who added that history repeats itself twice, the first time as tragedy and the second as farce. In this, as in so many things, Marx was an optimist. What he should have said is that history repeats itself many times, first as tragedy, then as farce, and forever after as etymology.

Take the word *jingoism*, a word that rehearses the whole history of British imperialism in miniature. It originated in 1878, in the political crisis over what the British called the Eastern Question. The Bulgarians had rebelled against their Turkish masters. The Turks suppressed the rising with terrible massacres and atrocities. In response, the Russian tsar declared war on the Turkish sultan in the name of his oppressed Slavic brethren, alarming the British, who had been watching Russia warily since the Crimean War of the early 1850s. That bloody exercise accomplished nothing, but it did enrich the English language. It gave us Tennyson's "Charge of the Light Brigade," not to mention the raglan sleeve and the cardigan sweater, named after the commanders who had ordered the brigade to glorious slaughter at the Russian batteries at Balaclava. Along with Wellington boots and the Eisenhower jacket, these items remind us of the great debt that haberdashery owes to generals.

But back to 1878. The tsar's troops advanced on Constantinople, and the British prepared to go to war. Queen Victoria told Prime Minister Disraeli she felt she couldn't remain "the Sovereign of a country that was letting itself down to kiss the feet of the great barbarians." Pro-war mobs took to the streets.

They broke windows at the house of the opposition leader William Gladstone, who wanted Britain to side with the Christian Bulgarians against the Turks. As their anthem they took the words of a popular music-hall song:

> We don't want to fight, but by jingo if we do,
> We've got the men, we've got the ships, we've got the money too.

And so the pro-war party came to be called the *jingoes* or *jingoists*.

Disraeli sent a British fleet to the Dardanelles. War was averted, however, when the sides signed a treaty at the Congress of Berlin in June 1878 and agreed to divide the spoils. The Russians got a couple of slices of Turkish territory, and the Turks got Bulgaria back after promising to treat the Christians more kindly. Britain, which had not fired a shot, got the island of Cyprus. Disraeli described the outcome with another phrase that would enter the language, as "peace with honor." But the British public was having second thoughts about abandoning the Turks. The affair became an issue in the 1880 elections, when Disraeli was turned out in favor of Gladstone, though the result may have owed as much to a national recession.

Gladstone was less bellicose than Disraeli, but that proved in turn to be *his* political undoing. In 1882 the celebrated General Gordon got himself besieged at Khartoum by the armies of the Islamic holy man known as the Mahdi. The jingoists resurfaced and demanded that a relief force be sent. But Gladstone temporized, unwilling to sacrifice British lives for a territory so inhospitable and remote. (When Ruskin first learned of the affair, he asked, "Who is the Sudan?") The relief force reached Khartoum three days too late to save Gordon; Gladstone's government was discredited and turned out of office.

Gordon's death was not avenged until fifteen years later,

when General Kitchener led an expedition that reconquered the Sudan and killed the Mahdi and ten thousand of his men. It was a famous victory, but its only contribution to English literature was Kipling's "Fuzzy-Wuzzy," which is hardly in a class with "The Charge of the Light Brigade." Neither Gordon nor Kitchener left his name on an article of clothing.

Linguistically, the pacific Mr. Gladstone probably came off best of anyone. The Gladstone bag is a suitcase divided into hinged compartments, a nice place to stow your kit once cooler heads prevail.

# A Suffix in the Sand   {1991}

TV announcers last week were referring to the inhabitants of Baghdad as *Baghdadis*. The word isn't in any English dictionary, but it sounds natural to add the *−i* suffix to the name of a city in that part of the world. It seems to form a pattern with *Iraqi, Kuwaiti, Saudi, Israeli, Pakistani, Bengali, Azerbaijani*, and the rest.

Still, it's a curious thing for English to do. We use a number of suffixes to form adjectives from the names of places, but none of the others is restricted to a particular area of the world. So we say *Japanese, Sudanese*, and *Portuguese; Irish, Polish*, and *Turkish*; and so on. But the suffix *−i* is used only for nations and regions that lie in the territory stretching from the Bible lands in the west to India in the east. Of course it isn't used for all the countries and regions in that area. For one thing, we attach *−i* only to the names of places that end in consonants, like Iraq and Kuwait; a person from Syria isn't a *Syri*. And for some countries in the region another suffix is used. People from Iran are *Iranians* and people from Afghanistan are *Afghans*—though I've heard *Irani* and *Afghani* or *Afghanistani* as well.

The immediate reason why the suffix *−i* is used for nations in this part of the world is that it comes from the languages spoken there. In Semitic languages like Arabic and Hebrew, the suffix *−i* is a way of forming adjectives out of nouns, like the English suffix *−ish* in words like *Polish, boyish*, or *fiendish*. The suffix was borrowed from Arabic into Persian, and from there into Urdu, an Indo-European tongue that's the language of modern Pakistan. It's from Urdu that we get words like *Pakistani, Punjabi*, and *Kashmiri*.

Still, this doesn't explain why English refers to these nationalities alone with a suffix taken from their native languages.

After all, this isn't something we do for peoples from other parts of the world. Why should we say *Iraqi* when we don't say *Italiano* or *Ruski* or *Nicaraguense*?

The explanation may lie in a history of colonial involvement that has given English speakers a special relationship with this region. The English use of the suffix −*i* began in the nineteenth century in India, in words like *Bengali* and *Punjabi*. Most likely it started with soldiers and colonial administrators who wanted to display a smattering of the local language to show that they were old India hands. Names like *Iraqi* and *Saudi* first appeared in the 1920s, when these nations were carved out of the parts of the former Ottoman Empire that had been known in the West as Mesopotamia and Arabia. (The name *Iraq* itself was taken from an archaic Arabic name for Babylon.) Here, too, the use of the native suffix suggested an intimacy with the local culture, in a time when T. E. Lawrence and Rudolph Valentino had turned the Arab into a figure of high romance. By the 1940s, the suffix had become a marker of Near Eastern provenance. When the modern state of Israel was founded, the word *Israeli* replaced the old form *Israelite*, though of course we still use *Israelite* to refer to the inhabitants of the ancient nation of Israel. (It's sort of like the distinction between *Grecian* and *Greek*.) And around the same time the old word *Yemenite* was dropped in favor of *Yemeni*.

The suffix −*i* draws its own kind of line in the sand. It circumscribes the region that Europeans used to refer to as the Orient, before that term was transferred to the Far East. As critics like Edward Said have pointed out, though, the Orient was a European invention. It has been imagined and reimagined in a line that runs from Flaubert and Kipling and Gérôme and Delacroix down to *Lawrence of Arabia* and *Raiders of the Lost Ark*. The Orient has been portrayed in varied and sometimes contradictory ways: it is despotic and devious, it is contemplative and mystical, it is languid and sensual, it is fanatical and puritanical. But it is always *the* Orient, a single place that blurs the vast differences in culture, history, and language which the region actually encompasses. In its own small way, the suffix *−i* contributes to the illusion. It doesn't just make Middle Easterners exotic; it makes them all exotic in the same dusky way.

# PC {1991}

In a speech at the University of Michigan commencement exercises not long ago, President Bush joined the fray over the "political correctness" issue on the nation's campuses. The President said that what began as "a crusade for civility" has turned into "Orwellian . . . crusades that demand correct behavior." He warned against what he called "attempts to micromanage casual conversation [that have] invited people to look for an insult in every word, gesture, action."

The phrase *politically correct* began its life as a bit of Marxist jargon. I suspect it was a direct translation of the German phrase *politisch korrekt*, but that may itself have been a translation of a Chinese phrase of Chairman Mao's. In any event, the English translation is a happy accident for the cultural right. In the original, the word *correct* meant simply "right" or "true," as it does in an English sentence like "Do you have the correct time?" — a nod to the doctrinaire Marxist view of history as an exact science. But the word has another meaning in English: when it's applied to social behavior, it suggests a conformity to superficial rules. You might ask which fork it's correct to use with the fish course, or whether it's correct to use *like* as a conjunction. But you probably wouldn't ask about the "correct" way to tell your son that you're disinheriting him. So when the phrase *politically correct* came into the English language, it implied that the doctrines at stake were mere matters of fashion. Rhetorically, it does the same work that *radical chic* did a generation ago: it drapes the cultural left in tie-dyed T-shirts.

Yet *correct* used to have a deeper moral sense. Carl Schurz described President Lincoln in 1864 as a man of "correct and firm principles," and Dickens had Mr. Dombey say that his first wife was a woman of "very correct feeling." That's a collocation that wouldn't come easily to modern English speakers, though in other languages the word is still used that way — the Frenchman's "Ce n'est pas correct" still has a ring of moral admonition.

As it happens, *correct* is just one of a family of words that have undergone the same kind of trivialization. Take the word *civility*. When Thomas De Quincey described the English universities in 1858 as "the recurring centers of civility," he didn't mean simply that the dons and students were courteous to one another, but that they preserved and refined the forms of conduct that were the basis of civilized society. And the word *polite* used to mean "refined" or "cultivated," a sense that survives only in fossilized phrases like "polite society" and "polite literature."

The word *manners* has probably suffered the most humiliating decline of all. Once it referred to general standards of moral conduct. That's what Tennyson had in mind when he wrote:

> Manners are not idle, but the fruit
> Of loyal nature and of noble mind.

Nowadays no one sees good manners as the fruit of noble anything. Nor is it a topic for poets or philosophers any longer. The great eighteenth-century works on manners were written by Lord Chesterfield and Voltaire. The most intelligent and thoughtful work on manners of the late twentieth century comes from an advice columnist who feels obliged to refer to herself in the third person and to camp herself up in a Victorian hairdo and a high-collared dress, lest anyone think she takes the subject too seriously. The word *manners* is like a Shakespearean actor who ends his career playing a butler on a TV sitcom. It might have been kinder to kill it off a century ago.

The writers of the Enlightenment made correctness and good manners one of the pillars of civil society. There is a story about Kant at the end of his life rising from his sickbed to bid a friend goodbye; when the friend told him there was no need to get up, the philosopher answered, "The feeling for humanity has not yet left me." Of course by the Victorian period the codes of social correctness had grown to Talmudic complexity. I suppose you could fairly describe them the way President Bush described modern standards of political correctness, as "attempts to micromanage conversation." And they led inevitably to the twentieth-century reaction, where outward forms were seen as trammels on the inner person; in the natural course of things, Emily Post set the stage for Mario Savio and Abbie Hoffman. Still, Matthew Arnold might be disconcerted to hear a conservative American president from a New England establishment family pronouncing the word *correctness* with a sneer.

# Party Down    {1996}

**A**t their convention last week the Republicans kept referring to themselves as the party of Lincoln, the way Republicans always do, but still there are certain Lincolnesque traits they would probably just as soon forget about. Long-windedness, among other things. Of course we remember Lincoln now as the author of those admirably pithy remarks given at Gettysburg in 1863. But at his 1858 debates with Douglas on the slavery question he spoke for four hours straight — this after Douglas had already spoken for three hours. And the audience hung around for all of it, maybe because they had little else better to do.

Those days are gone; this year the networks and the parties both have forgone even the pretense that Americans have the patience to listen to several hours of political oratory. Sometimes you had the feeling they'd prefer to abandon the whole form in favor of a more TV-friendly genre. The convention's most significant break with tradition might have been when Liddy Dole stepped down from the podium and wandered from delegate to delegate with a hand-held mike, in a style a lot more reminiscent of Phil Donahue than of Everett Dirksen.

Of course there had to be some speeches, but the organizers kept them very short and very bland, and the TV commentators evaluated them purely as performances; coming right on the heels of the Olympics, the broadcast could have made you think of a gymnastics or diving competition. A bunch of people come out and do pretty much the same routine, one after another, and then the networks cut to their booths, where an expert like Mark Shields or Kevin Phillips says something like "Well, Jim, he executed very nicely there with that line about empowerment — too bad he couldn't stick the peroration."

The only problem with this approach is that it's neither here nor there. When you watch the whole thing unfold on C-SPAN or PBS, it's a ragged affair that you just leave on in the background for a couple of hours while you cook dinner. As a one-hour TV show, though, it feels interminably long. Real TV shows don't have a single person talking for five minutes straight, much less five or six people in a row doing it, and no number of cutaways can make the program engaging. That's probably why all these attempts to turn the convention into a TV show have had the paradoxical effect of sharply lowering its ratings.

There's no going backwards to the days of Lincoln; the only thing is to cut the speeches still further. How far can they go with this? To find out, I got the texts of all the speeches from the first two nights of the Republican Convention, which came to around ten thousand words in all. Then I ran the whole thing through a piece of software developed by my colleagues at the Xerox Palo Alto Research Center, which produces an automatic summary of a text by analyzing word frequency, recurrent patterns, and so on. The program distilled the whole two nights of speechifying into five key sentences:

> We are the Republican Party — a big, broad, diverse, and inclusive party, with a commonsense agenda and a better man for a better America, Bob Dole. We need a leader we can trust. Thank you, ladies and gentlemen, for being part of this quest in working with us to restore the American dream. The commonsense Republican proposals are the first step in restoring the American dream because Republicans care about America. But there is no greater dream than the dreams parents have for their children to be happy and to share God's blessings.

I think you have to admit that the computer here has come up with as perfect a Republican convention speech as you are ever likely to hear.* Maybe the next time the Republicans convene they should consider having all their speakers give this same short speech as a kind of compulsory floor exercise. I don't mean everybody should have to say exactly the same words — this is America, after all. But you could give them each just one minute to hit on a certain number of obligatory themes and phrases: the American dream, God, family, good jobs, a great American.

That isn't really very different from what they're doing now, except that it's a lot more efficient for everybody. The convention organizers ensure that they get an even more uniform message across. The networks can shrink their present hour of prime-time coverage to half an hour. And commentators can concentrate on the execution of the speech without having to worry about minor variations in content — a level playing field at last.

---

* Not long after this piece aired, I tried the same experiment on the combined texts of the speeches from the first two nights of the Democratic convention in Chicago. In this case, though, the summarizer software returned pure word salad — maybe because Democrats have more trouble staying on message than Republicans do, maybe because they just go on longer.

# Standard Issue   {1997}

The Ebonics controversy is lurching into its second month with no letup in newspaper articles, editorials, and letters to the editor, almost all of them excoriating the Oakland school board for telling its inner-city students that they don't have to learn Standard English. In point of fact, the board did no such thing — all that the Oakland schools are actually asking their teachers to do is to take the students' own speech into account in teaching them the standard language. But the board's woolly and confused declaration about the program made this none too clear, and matters weren't helped when they chose to describe the language variety that their inner-city students speak as Ebonics, which sounds like the name of a sneaker or a 50s doo-wop group. And in any event, the press hasn't seemed interested in getting the facts right: it's too good a story the way they're telling it.

The columns and editorials have all hit more or less the same points. There are the denunciations of black speech, often in a tone of violent revulsion: "this appalling English dialect"; "a mutant language"; "gutter slang"; "the patois of America's meanest streets"; "the dialect of the pimp, the idiom of the gang-banger and the street thug, a form of pidgin English indicative of African-American failures." It's hard to read those characterizations without feeling that a current of displacement is at work — at least, it's striking how many of the words that critics apply to the dialect in the press are the same as the ones that many whites apply in private to the people who speak it. But prominent African-Americans, too, have been quick to condemn the school board — not just conservatives like Shelby Steele, but a range of figures from Kweisi Mfume to Kareem

Abdul-Jabbar. Apart from a few linguists and educators, most African-Americans seem to be unwilling to acknowledge that the inner-city variety might be a legitimate form of speech. And the Oakland parents and students sought out by enterprising reporters have been eager to deliver themselves of similar opinions. (From the *New York Times*: "'What's black English?' asked Mr. Andrews, a 16-year-old sophomore who said he found the [school board's] decision somewhat insulting. 'You mean slang?'")

But all that this shows is that middle-class blacks are as susceptible as anyone else to the conventional conception of African-American vernacular speech as slovenly and illogical — "a language that has no right or wrong expressions, no consistent spellings or pronunciations and no discernible rules," as William Raspberry described it in the *Washington Post*. Certainly no one, black or white, has been much interested in listening to the linguists who insist that the speech is in fact highly systematic (the absence of "consistent spellings" isn't surprising in a variety that is rarely written down). In the end, these judgments have less to do with racist stereotypes as such than with a kind of schoolroom lore that was current long before black speech could have been any kind of public issue. The critics are speaking not so much in the voice of David Duke as in the voice of their seventh-grade English teachers. You have the sense that the one unforgivable offense of the Oakland program is that it does not propose to tell its students that the way they speak is *wrong*.

But the press criticisms of the Oakland program aren't confused just in the way they talk about black English. There's an equally revealing confusion about the notion of "standard" English itself, as critics insist that the standard language's claim to legitimacy is not just practical and economic but moral and aesthetic as well. A *San Francisco Chronicle* editorial taxed the

Oakland school board with having "failed in its charge to teach youngsters their own language — epitomized by Shakespeare, the King James Bible and the writings of James Baldwin and Maya Angelou." A columnist in the *Los Angeles News* wrote, "What would have happened to the standard of excellence, if writers like Maya Angelou, James Baldwin, and Ralph Ellison had been told that all they needed to learn was black English?" And the syndicated columnist Ellen Goodman reminded the school board that "black English is not the language of Maya Angelou or Jesse Jackson." It seemed as if you couldn't open a newspaper last month without running into someone asking, "Why can't they all talk like that nice Ms. Angelou?"

Of course it's true that inner-city students don't speak the language of Maya Angelou and James Baldwin (though the rhythms of black street speech are a lot more audible in Angelou's poetry than the critics acknowledge). But then, upper-middle-class white students at high schools in Palo Alto and Greenwich, Connecticut, don't speak that language either (or, if you like, they don't speak the language of John Updike and Elizabeth Bishop, both credits to their race). The fact is that the language that kids in the Oakland schools need to learn in order to enter the cultural and economic mainstream has nothing to do with any of those high-flown models — it's the semigrammatical, jargon-strewn talk that you hear in corporate conference rooms or on the floor of Congress. Nobody in America ever had a career cut short for saying "between you and I" or using *impact* as a verb, and when corporate chiefs or government officials do find themselves in need of a little eloquence, they can just go out and hire it on the cheap. At a rough estimate, the ability to write correct and lucid English has a market value in modern America about one-third as great as the ability to install Windows on a PC.

Inner-city schools have a clear responsibility here, but it has nothing to do with "the language of Shakespeare." Their immediate task is to teach their charges to speak like kids in middle-class suburbs, so that they can grow up to become competent speakers of the brutalist clatter of the American political and business worlds. They don't have to talk like James Baldwin, but it is clearly to their advantage to be able to give a passable imitation of George Bush. (Maybe it would help to put a sign on the walls of all the Oakland classrooms: "If you leave out the verb, leave out the subject, too.")

Granted, that's not an easy task, for reasons that are partly linguistic and partly social. In the words of James Baldwin, that favorite model of Standard English probity, black children talk the way they do because "they refuse to be defined by a language that has never been able to recognize them." But the job will be easier if we forgo all those empty pieties about the moral and aesthetic superiority of the standard language. I'll grant you it would be nice if it didn't stop at that—we'd like to think the schools might actually be able to do something to raise the level of public language used by everybody. But that's another conversation, and there's no particular reason why it should begin in Oakland.

# Group Grope   {1998}

There was a curious sentence in the *New York Times* the other day in an article about the Senate maneuverings just before the Clinton trial: "The lawmakers... raised the allegation that Mr. Clinton groped Miss Willey." It took me aback to see that transitive use of the verb *grope* nestled in the midst of all the discreet formality of the *Times*. Of course that sexual sense of *grope* is perfectly good English — it has been around since Anglo-Saxon times, in fact. But it has lived all that time in the shadows of private life, and it's not a word we use when we're talking about sex in an official capacity.

I can understand, though, why the *Times* was led to use *grope* in this way. What other word could they have used? Merriam's defines *grope* in this sense as a synonym of *feel up*, but that one isn't fit to print either, at least not in a periodical that likes to style itself the newspaper of record. And while I suppose they could have gotten away with *fondle*, that doesn't have the same lubricious overtones. You can fondle your daughter's hair, but you couldn't very well grope it.

In a sense, this is what the whole Lewinsky affair keeps coming down to. From Clinton's own testimony to the Starr report to the presentations in the House committee and at the Senate trial, everybody keeps running aground on the problem of finding public language to talk about matters that belong exclusively to private life. That's what got Clinton in trouble in the first place — the difference between the public and private understandings of what it means when you say you had sex with someone. Technically speaking, you could say that Clinton was right to say that he used the words *sexual relationship* the way most Americans do. There was a big flap last week when the *Journal of the American Medical Association* published the results of a survey that showed that sixty percent of American adolescents refused to say that oral sex constituted having sex. (The journal's editor was forced to resign for interjecting the journal into a political controversy.) But it's hard to believe that this would come as a surprise to the members of Congress. They passed normal American adolescences, after all, and if you believe the press, more than a few of them have kept a hand in since then. You'd assume that they have native command of the American sexual vocabulary — *coming on, feeling up, doing it*, and of course the jog of the bases, first, second, and third. (We didn't ever mention crossing home plate when I was an adolescent, maybe out of superstition; it would have been like talking about a no-hitter while the game was still going on.)

But when we become parents with adolescents of our own we're obliged to disown these words, with the result that our public language leaves us with few resources for talking about sex as if we knew what was going on. Listening to the trial last week, I kept wishing someone would try to remind everyone what the story was really about. What if Charles Ruff had said to the senators, "Excuse me, but do the words 'going all the way' mean anything to you people?" But of course that wasn't about to happen. People can talk about the affair only in a mixture of clinical terms and circumlocutions, as if the matter under consideration were utterly alien to their experience — they sound like Eskimos trying to describe a surfing competition. The process reached its peak in the presentation by Bill McCollum of Florida, one of the House managers, who managed to use *genitalia* three times, *oral sex* three times, and *breasts* four times, excusing himself abjectly on each occasion.

It all wound up sounding far more prurient than any locker-room conversation. People have compared the Senate trial to a daytime talk show, but that has it all wrong. On *Jerry*

*Springer* they talk about sex in English words, the way any ordinary adolescent does, whereas when you listen to someone like McCollum you think of a hall monitor reporting to the principal on a couple he caught getting it on in the prom cloakroom. It's no wonder the public finds the whole business a turnoff (and let me say that it pains me deeply to have to use that term).

# The Jewish Question   {2000}

**I**f the Pulitzer committee gets around to awarding a prize for journalistic circumspection, it ought to give serious consideration to the way the *Washington Post* announced Gore's vice-presidential choice on August 7. The headline ran GORE TAPS LIEBERMAN AS RUNNING MATE, and the story went on to talk about Lieberman's political background for eleven paragraphs before it finally got around to noting that he was, as the *Post* demurely put it, "the first person of the Jewish faith selected to run on a national ticket" (a formulation that left open the possibility that there were atheistic Jews nominated before this).

The rest of the press was neither quite so restrained in its placement of the information nor quite so fastidious in conveying it. Actually the first I saw of the story was in a copy of the *San Francisco Examiner* that was sitting on a rack when I stopped at the corner store that morning. The headline screamed GORE PICKS JEWISH RUNNING MATE, and it was only when I squinted at the subhead that I found out that the vice-presidential candidate was going to be Senator Lieberman rather than, say, Larry King. That seemed an excessively prominent position to give the candidate's religion; I went around for the rest of the afternoon saying things to myself like "Men come to lay carpet for Jewish homeowner." Apparently the *Examiner* thought better of it, too — by the time the late edition came out, the headline had been changed to GORE'S HISTORIC PICK FOR VP, which at least left you equally in the dark as to who the choice was and why he was significant.

Most of the press tried to find a middle way between those extremes. The *New York Times*'s headline was LIEBERMAN WILL RUN WITH GORE, with the subhead FIRST JEW ON A MAJOR U.S.

TICKET. Even that got a number of people upset — some who were indignant about the prominence given to Lieberman's religion, and some who were just uncomfortable about seeing him baldly described as a Jew. It's odd to think that the word *Jew* can still summon up so much uneasiness, but that was evident in the number of circumlocutions and paraphrases that the press found for Lieberman, from the *Washington Post*'s "person of the Jewish faith" to the more common phrase "Jewish person," which I found in more than forty newspaper stories about Lieberman that appeared in the week following the announcement. I kept seeing things like "Will Americans vote for a Jewish person for vice-president?"

Why are people still diffident about calling somebody a Jew? It might be that the use of the word *Jew* as a noun is contaminated by its use as an attributive adjective, as in "Jew lawyer," "Jew banker," or "Jew shortstop." (That's not to mention the dazzlingly infelicitous phrase "Jew person," which was applied to Lieberman by the president of the Dallas chapter of the NAACP in the course of making some anti-Semitic remarks that promptly got him fired from his post.) And then there's the verb *to jew down*, which is clearly beyond the pale of polite conversation.

There should be nothing offensive about using *Jew* as a bare noun, but for more than a hundred fifty years that usage too has trailed a cloud of consternation behind it — ever since some people began to wonder whether anti-Semitism might be a social problem rather than an immutable part of the human condition. You can see the shift in the publishing history of Dickens' *Oliver Twist*. When the novel first appeared, in 1837, Fagin was described as a Jew in just about every sentence. "The Jew entered," "The Jew replied," "The Jew said" — it began to sound almost like a pronoun. But Dickens eliminated most of the occurrences of the word in later editions, probably in response to criticisms of the unsympathetic portrayal of Fagin. If he didn't actually change the character, he could at least draw less attention to his Jewishness.

Other nineteenth-century writers were even more leery of using the word *Jew*. The extreme case is Benjamin Disraeli's windy novel *Coningsby*, which describes its Jewish character Sidonia with every circumlocution available — he's an Israelite, then a Hebrew, then a Mosaic Arab. Or as Sidonia himself puts it to the young hero, "I am of that race that the Apostles professed before they followed your master." It's a description that makes the *Washington Post*'s "person of the Jewish faith" seem direct by comparison.

Not all authors were so fastidious, of course. George Eliot used *Jew* all the time in her 1876 novel *Daniel Deronda*, where she waded into the Jewish Question with a confidence bordering on chutzpah. That's the other tendency you could see in the press reaction to the Lieberman choice. If the *Washington Post*'s circumspection had an opposite number, it was in *Time* magazine's decision to entitle its cover story on Gore's choice "Chutzpah!" The word was lifted from Lieberman's quip that some people might describe his selection as an act of chutzpah. The article helpfully translated the word as "audacity," but actually it's a lot closer to "nerve" or "effrontery." In Lieberman's mouth it might be self-mockery, but coming from *Time* it gave the impression that the nomination was an outrage — almost certainly not what they wanted to convey. In its own small way, the headline was a bungled act of chutzpah all by itself.

# Only Contract   {2000}

I know what I'd tell Al Gore if I were an advisor concerned about people's perception of him as stiff and formal. Just two words: "Only contract!" When you're listening to the debate tonight, count how many times Gore contracts *have* or *be* when the context would allow it. In the first two debates he was doing it only about forty-five percent of the time. He doesn't just pronounce every word, he pronounces the spaces between. "That — is — wrong. We — have — got — to — balance — the — budget."

This is not a problem for George W. Bush. The man contracts — between eighty-five and ninety percent of the time, when the verb isn't emphasized. Words like *I'm* and *there's* — I'm not sure if Bush even knows they have apostrophes in them. For Bush, *going to* is invariably pronounced *gonna*, or even *monna*, as in "I monna trust em." And Gore's *we have got to* always shows up in Bush's mouth as *we gotta*: "We gotta ban partial-birth abortions," "We gotta make sure our seniors get the promise made." Of course everybody uses *gotta* informally, but in a televised debate it's what actors like to call a choice. (When I looked up the transcript of the debate the next day on the CNN website it turned out they'd changed most of Bush's *gotta*s to *need to*s. That's a legitimate edit, since "we gotta" looks pretty rough on the page. But Gore doesn't need those editorial cleanups.)

The speech differences are all the more striking when you consider that we've never had two presidential candidates whose linguistic backgrounds were so similar, at least on the face of things. Bush and Gore both grew up in Washington political families, spent their youth going back and forth between Southern states and Northeastern prep schools, and went to Ivy

League universities before returning home. Unlike the other Southerners who have run for national office in the last fifty years, both men came by their accents in a more or less conscious way.

If we want to explain the differences, then, we'd have to start way back, or way deep. Maybe it begins with the fathers whom the sons were named for. Senator Albert Gore Senior was the son of a hardscrabble farmer from Possum Hollow, Tennessee. That was country before country was cool, and by all accounts Gore Senior was highly self-conscious about his language: he practiced his elocution and used words he found in the dictionary. As a famously demanding father, it isn't likely he would have tolerated any *gonna*'s or *gotta*'s around the family dinner table. It's a fastidiousness that Al Junior finds it hard to break with. He can cultivate that accent and make a sedulous effort to drop his *g*'s, but people still find it difficult to get his name into the same sentence as the word *homespun*, and nobody is ever going to refer to him as Tennessee Al.

Al Gore Senior is a far cry from George Herbert Walker Bush, himself the son of a senator from a patrician Connecticut family. As a young man, it's true, George W. had ambivalent feelings about assuming that New England mantle of *noblesse oblige*, and that youthful rebellion is evident in his extravagant embrace of Texas vowels. His accent is a lot thicker than his brothers'. In fact, the other day I was listening to a C-SPAN rebroadcast of the 1988 vice-presidential debate, and I was struck by how much thicker Bush's accent is than Lloyd Bentsen's. But Bentsen didn't have anything to prove — he was born and educated in Texas, not Connecticut (a point that's elided on the Bush for President website).

But George W. got one linguistic legacy from his father that didn't have to be altered for a new climate — his nonchalant ungrammaticality. It's the hallmark of the old WASP establishment, a class that regards taking pains with language as the unerring signal of someone who is trying too hard. As it turns out, it was a happy accident for Dubya. The tousled syntax that served the Bushes well at Andover and Kennebunkport turned out to be just the thing for campaigning in west Texas — none of them places that value an excessive attention to subject-verb agreement. "There's a lot of procedures that have not kept up.... There's no prescription drug benefits, there's no drug therapies, there's no preventing medicines."

Of course Bush Junior sometimes tries to rise to the occasion, the same way Gore Junior tries to sink to it. When Dubya wants to sound presidential, he'll try to construct a sentence that suggests some sense of mission, what his father used to call "the vision thing." But it's like someone assembling a barbecue — when the sentence is finished there are always a half-dozen parts left over.

It's odd that neither candidate has been able to overcome those early influences. It gives you a new appreciation for politicians who have that capacity to create a resonant public voice while preserving the illusion of intimate speech. Clinton does it brilliantly, of course. And so did Reagan — his syntax might have been shaky on occasion, but unlike either of the Bushes he usually got to the end of his sentences around the same time the period did. When you see how difficult it is for the present candidates to achieve that effect, you realize how early in life Clinton's and Reagan's self-fashioning must have begun. I don't know where that gift comes from, but it probably doesn't help to have a strong father.

# Chad Row {2000}

**W**hat an odd career the word *chad* has had — decades spent sinking into obscurity, then an unexpected last moment in the sun. Just a couple of weeks ago it was an item that Regis Philbin might have thrown at you when you got to five hundred thousand dollars; now it's one of those two-hundred-dollar gimmes that he asks just to make sure everybody goes home with carfare.

The origins of the word are lost in the murky prehistory of interface design. One suggestion is that it comes from a Scottish dialect word for "loose stones or gravel" and originated with British codebreakers during World War II — a nice romantic touch. Or it's an acronym for "Card Hole Aggregate Debris" (but that's a game anybody can play — why not "Comes Hanging and Dimpled"?). And then there's the theory that *chad* comes from the Chadless Keypunch. As the story goes, that device was originally named after its inventor, but since it didn't produce confetti-like pieces of paper the way other keypunches did, people assumed that the name meant "without chad." It's an etymology worthy of the programmers who contrived it, and it seems churlish to note that there is no record of there ever having been an inventor named Chadless.

In any event, there's no way to know. The first print citations for the word date from the mid-1940s, but that's not always a reliable indicator of when a word was first used, and *chad* could go back much further than that. After all, those little bits of paper have been around for a long time — the path of history is strewn with the stuff. The word could have been coined by E. S. Votey around the time he patented the paper-tape system for his player piano in 1897. Or it could have begun with Dr. Herman Hollerith, the Census Bureau employee who had the idea for the first punch-card tabulating machine in the 1880s when he saw a conductor punching a train ticket, and went on to found a little company that eventually become IBM. Or perhaps it goes back to Joseph-Marie Jacquard, who first used interchangeable punched cards in automatic looms just after the French Revolution — an invention that incited a riot among the silk weavers of Lyon, in the first political conflict that we can definitely ascribe to punch-card technology.

What's interesting isn't where the word comes from, though, but that we're still using it now. By all rights *chad* ought to be obsolete, along with the technology it came in with. Most punch-card machines were scrapped long ago — election boards have been able to prolong their life because they bring them out for just one day a year, when they emerge from the mists of the past like a digital Brigadoon.

In fact, everything that went on last week had a decidedly retro feel. For a moment, we were reliving that first moment when the computer began to make itself felt in American life — the age of number-two black pencils, punch cards, and those kinky injunctions not to fold, spindle, or mutilate. It was the golden age of chad, a time of boundless faith in the powers of digital technology. The descendants of Dr. Hollerith's machines were everywhere, as the company he founded sent out legions of crew-cut missionaries to preach the gospel of machine efficiency. Business would be rationalized, machine-graded standardized tests would ensure a perfect meritocracy.

James Baker caught the spirit of that age perfectly in his paeans to the "precision machinery" that delivers us from human error and subjectivity. It's true that other Republicans were making the same argument about the superiority of machine counting, but Baker's invocation of "precision machinery" was another oddly retro note, as if he thought Americans would still feel confident about trusting their future to the reliability of any device equipped with a paper feeder. But then, Baker is probably one of the few people whose visions of technology haven't been sullied by having to interact with it — like his former boss President Bush, who marveled at bar codes when he first encountered them in a visit to a supermarket trade show during the 1992 presidential campaign.

This is sure to be the *Liebestod* of *chad*; within a couple of years the word will be as obscure a curiosity as *boy toy* or *pet rock*. The last punch-card tabulators will be consigned to museums of technology alongside the hurdy-gurdy and the Jacquard loom, and everyone will move on to voting with more sophisticated technology. All in all, it's probably a good thing. Electronic voting is cleaner and more accurate, and less prone to the random disturbances that the signal-processing people call noise. But of course no voting method is perfect. Internet voting disenfranchises the digitally disadvantaged and is sure to be disrupted by server crashes and new forms of election fraud. The only difference is that next time we won't be treated to all those images of election officials squinting at bits of paper — images that at least serve to remind us what all those utopian fantasies of technological precision come down to in the end. That's the great advantage of the punch-card machine: at least you can hear the noise it makes.

# the two R's

# I Put a Spell on You    {1990}

Yୱou will have heard that America is currently in the throes of a literacy crisis: workers can't read instruction manuals, managers can't write a simple memo. Hence the clamor for a "return to basics." But few people have interpreted this rallying cry quite so literally as William Olsten, the chairman of a large temporary-help agency. With the cooperation of a number of companies, the Olsten Corporation last week held the second in a series of regional spelling bees for grownups, in Secaucus, New Jersey. The winner was a forty-year-old mental-health counselor who walked away with an all-expenses-paid vacation in Curaçao.

The spelling bee is a curious American custom, one of the last vestiges of nineteenth-century education preserved in a pure form. No other nation has anything like it, not even the British, who wrestle with the same spelling system as we do. But to think of it as primarily a device for providing people with basic literacy skills is sort of like thinking of the Japanese tea ceremony as a means of providing people with liquid nourishment. The spelling bee is a ritual performance.

At one level you can take the spelling bee as a model for how the process of selection is supposed to work in democratic education. Nothing is fairer than a spelling test, after all. The rules are the same for everyone: there is no cultural bias, no subjectivity about right and wrong answers. And unlike other subjects, spelling gives no special advantage to those children who happen to be brighter or more creative than their classmates. The wonderful thing about English spelling—at the fourth-grade level, anyway—is that it makes no sense at all. A powerful intellect and a vivid imagination are no help when it comes to figuring out that it's *i* before *e* in *friend* and the other way round in *weird*. In spelling, at least, you and I walk arm in arm with Henry James. There may be such a thing as a natural bent for spelling, but God appears to have distributed that gift blindly, with a perfectly even hand.

In fact, the spelling bee is specifically designed to detach spelling from the practical skills you need for reading and writing. You don't have to be able to understand the word when you read it in context; you don't have to know how to use it in a sentence. Last year, the national student spelling bee was won by a kid who nailed down his victory by spelling the word *ratatouille*. This is an extraordinary accomplishment, all the more so because it involves such a sublimely useless bit of knowledge. With only average luck, after all, you can go through an entire literate life without ever having to write the word *ratatouille*. I was disappointed to hear that some of the other contestants had protested the win, on the grounds that *ratatouille* isn't really an English word. The fact is that the best spelling-bee words are never really English. They're dictionary words like *viridescent* and *innominate* and *mythopoeia*, the sorts of words we keep around only to keep spelling bees in business. (The words that win spelling bees are always much too long to be helpful for Scrabble, the other field of play for useless lexical information.)

What's even stranger is that the spelling bee is an entirely oral ritual—you could run the whole procedure in the dark. In theory, I suppose, somebody could win a spelling bee without knowing how to read or write at all, the way some toddlers can tell you how to spell their name without being able to write it down. As it happens, the spelling bee originated at a time when children were taught in just this way. They learned spelling as a purely oral skill before they started reading. As one influential educator put it in 1827, "It is quite useless to put a child to reading till he can spell and pronounce, without aid, the syllables and words he must meet with." Or, in the words of an early primer:

> And if you can't read pray endeavor to spell,
> For by frequent spelling you'll learn to read well.

But reading has not been taught this way for more than a hundred years, and yet the spelling bee survives. One reason for its enduring appeal, I suspect, is that it invokes the sense of mystery that attached to writing before the age of widespread literacy. When I think of those kids chanting the spellings of words like *ratatouille* and *viridescent*, I can't help recalling that *spell* also refers to a magical formula or incantation. The two senses are related: the connection goes back to a time when written words were invested with magical power.

There's something compelling about this notion of the talismanic power of the written word, especially for third- and fourth-graders. But most of us grow out of it sooner of later. I'm always a little embarrassed to meet grownups who takes an inordinate pride in their ability to spell well, but that might be sour grapes. When I was a kid, I was always sent to my seat in an early round when I blew the second vowel of *separate*.

# Naming of Parts   {1994}

Around twenty years ago, the psychologist Stanley Milgrim did a study of the mental maps that New Yorkers construct of their city. He showed people photographs of various parts of the city and asked them where they thought the pictures were taken. It turned out that when they weren't sure, they tended to say, "I don't know, what is that, Queens?"

The adverb is the Queens of grammar. What do you do with the word *ago*, for example? It's obviously not a noun or a verb, and it doesn't feel much like an adjective. It can't be a preposition, because everybody knows that preposition means "put before," and *ago* is put after. So put it in the adverb pile — nobody ever looks there anyway. And indeed that's how it's labeled in every dictionary, along with a bunch of other words that seem to have nothing at all in common: *quickly* and *very* and *aboard* and *nonetheless*. The dictionaries even tell you that the word *the* is an adverb in a phrase like "the more the merrier."

It sounds like something out of a story you could imagine Borges writing, one about a medieval encyclopedia that groups all the animals into four classes: the ones that walk, the ones that crawl, the ones that jump, and the ones that burrow, fly, or swim. And in fact the story we learn in school about the parts of speech is a vestige of the grammatical theory of the early Middle Ages, where the parts of speech were keys to God's ordained order of things. Philosophically, the view went underground around the time of Pierre Abelard and William of Ockham, but it has survived over the succeeding eight centuries in the oral lore of the classroom.

We linguists have our own modern theories of grammar,

with their own exotic categories. *The* is a determiner, *ago* is a postposition, *nonetheless* is a sentential adjunct. But educators and even lexicographers prefer the categories they learned in school. And I suppose I can understand their point of view. After all, the study of grammar has always been invested with a mysterious power to shape the mind and the soul. One nineteenth-century educator called grammar "an employment calculated to exclude those frivolous pursuits, and that love of ease and sensual pleasure, which enfeeble and corrupt the minds of many inconsiderate youth, and render them useless to society." And in fact there are people who maintain that the de-emphasis of grammar in the schools was responsible for all the social tumult of the 60s and 70s. As the headmaster of the Westminster School put it a couple of years ago, "As nice points of grammar were mockingly dismissed as pedantic and irrelevant, so was punctiliousness in such matters as honesty, responsibility, property, gratitude . . . and so on."

From the linguists' point of view, it's true, school grammar can seem an exercise in the absurd: you take an arbitrary set of premises and follow them through to their conclusions, come what may. Consider the sort of reasoning you have to go through to come up with the conclusion that *the* is an adverb in a phrase like "the more the merrier." You say, Well, *more* is an adjective, and *the* modifies *more*, and an adverb is anything that modifies a verb or an adjective or another adverb, so *the* must be an adverb here. If you were looking at this with the cool eye of science, you'd say, Gee, maybe there's something wrong with that theory. But this sort of grammatical reasoning is just the sort of thing you need to endure the trials of ordinary experience. You call up the airline and you say, "Look, if you charge five hundred and fifty for a flight from San Francisco to Atlanta that stops in Dallas, I don't see how you can charge seven hundred dollars just to fly the San Francisco–Dallas leg." And if they have their wits about them they answer you, "Well, with all respect, sir, you're no grammarian."

Nietzsche saw all the tricks of grammar and despaired of them. "Reason in language — oh, what a deceptive old woman she is!" he said. "I am afraid that we'll never get rid of our belief in God because we still have faith in grammar." But of course that's just why the defenders of the old order cling to traditional grammar so tenaciously. Let people once doubt the reality of adverbs and it's only a short step to doubting the reality of the most basic categories of experience — God, excursion fares, the borough of Queens.

# Reading for the Plot   {1994}

**E**ighteenth-century philosophers like Hume held that nature endows everyone with an innate little kernel of taste, which grows with cultivation. Until a while ago my five-year-old showed no signs of having any such organ. She eschewed Big Bird for a halfwit dinosaur who sings treacly songs about dental hygiene and moved on from there to the Mighty Morphin Power Rangers.

Then all of a sudden something seemed to germinate. In the car about a month ago she asked me to put the Elvis tape on, and when I did and it started to play "It's Now or Never," she threw a fit and said she wanted to hear the one about the hound dog. And now she has conceived a sudden passion for the tales of Beatrix Potter.

History hasn't been very generous to Potter, at least by comparison with her near-contemporary A. A. Milne. One reason is doubtless that most people have trouble getting past the Laura Ashley–style illustrations and the cloying names of her characters: Benjamin Bunny, Timmy Tiptoes, and of course Peter Rabbit's celebrated siblings, Flopsy, Mopsy, and Cotton-tail. In fact, though, Potter's tales have none of the preciousness you find in Milne. I always have the feeling that the Pooh stories were written so that grownups would find them darling. But Potter is an uncompromising naturalist, with a wryness that leaves her tales always coming out a little equivocal. Her stories are populated by real-life folk who fret about their livelihoods and get themselves caned and occasionally wind up as somebody else's dinner.

There is no condescension in Potter's language, either. The other night, for example, we were reading "The Tale of Johnny Town-Mouse," a version of Aesop's story of the country mouse and the city mouse that Potter turns into a contemporary fable. Johnny Town-mouse is an Edwardian dandy with a long tail and a white necktie who dines on the scraps of the elegant upstairs dishes, and who talks a good deal like somebody in a Saki story. When the country mouse says he must return home, Johnny says, "I confess I am a little disappointed; we have endeavoured to entertain you, Timothy William." I'm not sure whether even an Edwardian five-year-old would have made sense of that; in any case, it must have flown right over Sophie's head. She lay there with her eyes fixed in the middle distance, looking over every once in a while to check out the pictures, and playing with the string of a Barney balloon she'd gotten at a birthday party earlier in the day. I read on to the part where the city mouse visits the country mouse, who asks after his old friends. "Johnny's account was rather middling. He explained why he was paying his visit so early in the season; the family had gone to the sea-side for Easter; the cook was doing spring cleaning, on board wages, with particular instructions to clear out the mice." *Middling*? *Board wages*? I looked over at Sophie, but she was still lying there, abstractedly twirling the string of her balloon. Maybe it doesn't matter, I thought. Maybe it's like the structuralists say: literature is just the play of empty signifiers. I read on: "There were four kittens, and the cat had killed the canary." Sophie sat up with a start: "What's a canary?"

That's what's meant by reading for the plot. And of course she got it absolutely right. All very nice about the sea-side and the cook, but when it comes to the crunch it's the cat you want to keep your eye on. Just like everything else in childhood, listening in on all those incomprehensible conversations and trying to figure out what it really comes down to. The process is supposed to get easier as time goes by, as people acquire what E. D. Hirsch calls cultural literacy — the background information that you need to have to make sense of what you're reading. Yet Sophie seems untroubled by her deficient grasp of the culture and language of Edwardian England. It reminds you that the books that have mattered most to you are the ones that were too hard for you at the time. You think of the first time you read James or Joyce, tearing through paragraph after paragraph in rapt incomprehension. And who do you think gets more out of "The Tale of Johnny Town-Mouse," Sophie or me?

# Split Decision   {1995}

**N**ot long ago somebody sent me a handsome brochure that had been published by the communications department of a large corporation to tell employees how to write more effectively. It was the third of these things that I've seen, and it's fair to conclude that corporate America has some sense that there's a problem here. Of course you could say that asking a corporate communications department to look after the state of English usage is sort of like putting the fox in charge of the henhouse. But these people have their hearts in the right place, even if they do have a few feathers sticking out of the corners of their mouths. Specialists in effective communication themselves, they've tried to distill their wisdom on the topic into a handful of high-value rules that busy people can take in quickly. For example, the guide says, "Make sure the right words are next to each other." That's as close to a golden rule of writing as anything I've seen, even if it leaves you a little hazy on the details. But none of these guides ever gets so general that it leaves out the dictum to "avoid splitting infinitives." That's the one rule that is likely to survive when all the rest of grammar has withered away.

The split-infinitive rule was dreamed up by grammar-book writers in the middle of the nineteenth century and has been handed down since then by generations of schoolteachers. Nobody has ever given a good justification for it. It isn't logical, and it doesn't make writing clearer; quite the contrary. "We are planning to aggressively seek well-tested solutions" — rewrite that with the adverb anywhere else and you'll wind up with an ambiguous sentence. There are some cases, in fact, where the language gives you no choice but to split. How would you avoid the construction in a sentence like "The treatment seems to more than double the rate of cure"? "The treatment seems more than to double . . . "? I don't think so.

Most of the best grammarians have recognized the split-infinitive rule for the flimflam it is. H. W. Fowler described people who followed the rule as "bogey-haunted creatures . . . whose aversion springs not from instinctive good taste, but from tame acceptance of the opinion of others." Wilson Follett insisted in his *Modern American Usage* not only that split infinitives were called for on occasion, but that "desk sets should include small hatchets of silver or gold for the purpose." And in their *Dictionary of Contemporary American Usage,* Bergen and Cornelia Evans included a long list of notable splitters running from Wordsworth, Coleridge, and Byron to Henry James, Thomas Hardy, and George Bernard Shaw. Actually Shaw once wrote to a publisher whose proofreader had rashly corrected a split infinitive in his prose and said, "I call for the immediate dismissal of [this] pedant. . . . It is of no concern to me whether he decides to go quickly or to quickly go."

But the people who write the corporate guides to effective writing don't give much evidence of having paid attention to books like these. Fowler, Follett, and the rest are wordy tomes full of explanations, exceptions, and equivocations that make grammar seem a much more complicated business than a busy modern writer can be expected to take time for. The writers of these guides are the office grammarians, the people who take pleasure in calling themselves sticklers. What they have is not the sense they were born with, exactly, but some dim memories of the sense they learned at the end of Sister Petra's ruler in sixth grade. And Sister Petra and the split-infinitive rule were made for each other. It is one of the pure mysteries of grammar, a mirror of those other, higher mysteries that it is given only to Sister Petra and her acolytes to fully understand.

The whole history of grammar has been a long struggle between the Fowlers and the Sister Petras of this world. The great irony is that now it's the new technologies of writing that are ensuring the victory of the good sister's side. She and her charges were merely hostile to reason, but the grammar checker that's bundled with your word processor is physically incapable of it. It's in the nature of the technology that the rules become simplified and automated, with the complexities and subtleties relegated to the margins. And the fact is that any software house selling a grammar checker that didn't flag split infinitives would find itself cut off from a huge part of its market.

Some people will say that the corporate brochures and the grammar checkers are just one more instance of the dumbing down of America, but Sister Petra wouldn't put it that way. She'd say that we're merely moving the grammar to a higher plane of pure observance.

# Sex and the Singular Verb {1996}

**A**lice has her feminist credentials so squarely in line that she can get away with reading anything. "You want to look at this month's *Cosmopolitan*," she told me. "They have a grammar quiz in there." I told her I'd pick it up, asked her what was on the cover. She snorted. "It's *Cosmopolitan*," she said. "What do you think is on the cover?"

I found the quiz anyway, in the back of the April issue, between a feature on Heather Locklear and an ad for an exercise video called *Buns of Steel*. "How good is your grammar?" the header said. "That pretty little mouth of yours may not always say the correct thing." I figured it was going to be one of those dress-for-success things. But most of the sentences in the test had nothing to do with the language that that *Cosmopolitan* girl might use in a job interview. They were written in the sassy dialect that *Cosmo* likes to imagine its readers use with each other when they're touching up their blush in the ladies' room. Can you spot the grammatical errors in the following? "Between you and I, I think Marci and John are sleeping together." "The madness of the affair — furtive kisses, secret phone calls, weekend getaways — are what really appealed to her." "I can swing the Todd Oldham dress if my mother loans me the money." "Any chance of him meeting us after the Pearl Jam concert?" "I'm going to St. Kitts. Which bikini do you think I should bring with me?" (Actually I had to think twice about that one, since like most New Yorkers I've always been a little fuzzy on the *bring-take* business.) The quiz had the lubricious tone of every other feature in the magazine; I half expected to come to the end and find something like "Add up your score. If you got more than twelve, you are multiorgasmic."

It's a curious incongruity. When you think about grammar,

you think of a gray, neutered place whose streets are lined with neoclassical façades. It's the North Korea of language, not a place I ordinarily think of that *Cosmopolitan* girl as hanging out in. I think of her as someone who uses *like* as a conjunction, says *ain't* when she feels like it, and swears while she's trying to light up in a convertible. Still, why shouldn't she indulge in a little correct grammar now and then? A nice touch, like linguistic lip-liner. I can hear the magazine now. "Just the thing to keep him interested. That pretty little mouth of yours drawn in a pout as it closes around a *whom*. That coy overture when he calls you from a pay phone: 'My roommates are all at the beach. The only one here is little old I.'"

Indeed, why not? After all, grammar's gotten to be a pretty dreary business. We seem to have lost sight of the fact that the word is related to *glamour*, via an old Scottish word that means "sorcery." Maybe that's just the fate grammar deserves, to become so arcane and retro that it starts to sound kinky. It seems a natural for a decade that's seen the revival of the Wonderbra and the corset — a hint of uplift, a soupçon of constraint. Now *there's* an idea for an MTV video, Madonna in a merry widow singing, "I am a grammatical girl." And thank goodness we still have Helen Gurley Brown around to write a sequel to her 60s bestseller; she can call this one *Sex and the Singular Verb*.

# Verbed Off  {1997}

"**I** don't think we should wordsmith this in public." That was the response of Joseph Cammerata, at the time one of Paula Jones's attorneys, when someone asked him about the possibility of a settlement on *Meet the Press*. It's the sort of usage that language critics love to jump on; nothing raises the ire of the correcting classes so readily as these shifts from nouns to verbs. Even the comic strips' Calvin got his two cents in a while ago; as he put it, "Verbing weirds language."

Actually, though, it isn't that easy to say why the noun-to-verb business gets such a bad rap. The linguist Steven Pinker has estimated that fully twenty percent of English verbs began their lives as nouns. You can face the enemy, nose around the office, mouth the lyrics, shoulder the burden, elbow your way in, finger the culprit, knuckle under, foot the bill, toe the line. You can milk the cow, in which case you remove some liquid, or milk the veal, in which case you add it.

And it's true that the language adds new coinages like these every day, with most of them passing unnoticed. The verb *to telephone* was introduced just four years after Alexander Graham Bell patented his new invention, and since then it's been joined by the verbs *to radio, to FedEx, to fax, to keyboard*, and dozens of others, with nobody raising an eyebrow.

You have to admit, too, that the process can give rise to new and colorful coinages. Not long ago I was reading a novel by Bruce Olds where he talked about blood roostertailing from a wound. It was a pretty graphic effect, and one you could never achieve in a language like French or Italian, which doesn't permit this sort of syntactic switch-hitting.

But not all the new coinages have that macabre charm.

When you listen to corporate managers, you could be put in mind of a language like Eskimo, where words can migrate freely from one part of speech to another. "We have a team partnering with IBM that is tasked with architecting the new standards. They've been officing across the street but they conference down the hall."

Still, maybe it's wrong to single out corporations as the chief perpetrators here. I did a search of a humanities and social science database and found more than four thousand citations of the new use of the verb *privilege*, as in "realism privileges interiority." Psychologists have been talking a lot lately about journaling — a process a lot like keeping a diary, only with a spiritual dimension that's absent in old-style diarists like Boswell or Gide. And Baptists, Pentecostals, and the like have managed to make a verb out of the noun *fellowship*, as in "I fellowship at the Assembly of God on Winchester Avenue." (I ran into a news story a while ago about a woman who was disfellowshipped from a Texas Church of Christ after her husband divorced her. Since then I keep expecting the verb to turn up in a letter from the MasterCard people.)

But what makes these usages fishy, when no one troubles over most other shifts of nouns to verbs? You often hear people say that the new verbs don't add anything to the language, but I suspect the problem is that they do: they come with a presupposition that any activity worth mentioning ought to have a verb of its own. And even though the noun-to-verb pattern has been around a long time, there does seem to be something in this urge to verb that's a genuine novelty on the linguistic scene.

You hear it not just in corporate or academic jargon but in everyday speech. The night before Diana's funeral I heard a newscaster on the BBC talking about crowds of people vigiling outside Buckingham Palace. The Book-of-the-Month Club features a book called *Classy Knitting: A Beginner's Guide to*

*Creative Sweatering.* An NYU psychologist gives the following advice for home redecoration: "Don't think about the bedroom — a static concept. Instead, think of bedrooming." It occurs to you that people have been knitting sweaters for a couple of thousand years now and doing whatever they do in bedrooms for longer than that, but they've never before felt the need to turn the nouns into verbs to denote those activities. But maybe it's no less than our active lifestyles deserve. That's what modern life feels like, just one damn thing after another — breakfasting, carpooling, officing, keyboarding, Stairmastering, journaling, bedrooming. Why shouldn't we wordsmith new ways to talk about it?

# Hell in a Handcar   {1999}

**B**eing bearish isn't always a very successful strategy in the stock market, but in the language market it's always a sure thing. At any time in the past four hundred years you could claim that the language was falling apart, in full confidence that you'd never get called to cover your short positions. From Jonathan Swift to the current crop of language pundits, commentaries on the state of the language have been an unbroken stream of jeremiads and complaints.

When you take the history of complaints as a whole, it can be a little perplexing. Surely those bears couldn't all have been right or we'd be reduced by now to communicating in ursine grunts. But none of that shakes the faith of the current generation of critics. And to tell the truth, I have the same impression myself. I look around me and the signs seem unmistakable that the language is in a bad way. I'm not talking about the arcane rules of grammar that tell you when to use *each other* and *one another*, or what the difference is between *in behalf of* and *on behalf of*. Nobody knows those rules anymore, not even the copy editors at the *New York Times*. But people seem to have lost their grip even on the simple things, like when to write *its* without an apostrophe.

But are things really worse than they used to be? Maybe it's just that I'm getting old and cranky. The fact is, complaining about English usage has always been an old man's game (and I mean *man*— *curmudgeon* is not a word we use of women). And it occurs to me that maybe there was just as much of this going around twenty or thirty years ago, but that I was merely too callow to notice it, or too mellow to care.

It would be a hard point to prove one way or the other. We

don't actually expect the people who complain about the state of the language to document their claims, the way we would if they were economists. "The pronoun *whom* was off sharply last quarter, as the language was already reeling from a 37 percent increase in the use of *office* as a verb in fiscal 1998." Critics just assume that most people knew how to write and spell correctly until things started to fall apart a generation or so ago.

But maybe this is just an effect of the selectivity of literary memory. Whatever becomes of the general run of evil that men do, their bad writing is usually interred with their bones. We don't have to read the interoffice memos or popular journalism of earlier generations, just as our descendants will be spared reading ours. It can come as a shock when you rummage through a pile of old magazines at a garage sale and realize that the *Saturday Evening Post* was a lot worse written than *People* is. For that matter, we tend to forget how bad our own writing used to be.

And yet something *has* been changing over the years. It isn't that people are writing worse but that they're writing more, and spreading it about more widely. It's the effect that Jacques Barzun described fifty years ago as the endless multiplication of dufferism. On a per capita basis, we aren't producing many more novels or histories than we were in the eighteenth century. But there has been a huge growth in sectors like popular magazines, government pamphlets, press releases, and user manuals — most of them written by people who would not have been putting pen to paper in the age of Johnson.

The Internet is just the latest development in this process. People keep pointing out that the wonderful thing about the Net is that anybody can post a message and reach a potential audience of millions. And anybody has been doing exactly that. The number of people who sit down at a keyboard every day has probably increased tenfold over the past few years — quite a few of them people whose writing used to be seen only on their refrigerator doors. They're people who were never able to spell very well, but over the telephone you couldn't tell.

There are two ways to think about this. On the one hand, you could say that writing was generally better when there were fewer people doing it, the way major-league pitching was better before league expansion. On the other, there has never been an age when the average person has written so much, or so well. Writing is like whistling, after all — the more people practice, the better they get. But even with the broad indexes up, I wouldn't look for any analyst upgrades in this sector.

# Distinctions  {2000}

Some years ago I had dinner with the distinguished British lexicographer Edward Weiner. At the time he was the editor of the *Oxford English Dictionary*, but before that he had also edited a usage book for Oxford. As it happened, I had just finished writing the usage material for a new edition of the *American Heritage Dictionary*, so we fell to comparing notes, as it were. He asked me why I had taken it on. I told him I did it in the hope that I'd finally master the difference between *in behalf of* and *on behalf of*. "Didn't work, did it?" he said. I confessed that it hadn't — I still couldn't remember which was which. "Me neither," he said, and then he leaned over to me in a conspiratorial way. "You know, if neither of us can keep this one straight, why don't we just quietly agree to bag it?"

I wonder if we could have gotten away with it. Certainly we're not the only ones who aren't clear on this rule. The grammar books tell you that you should use *on behalf of* when one person is acting as agent for another, as in "She made the offer on behalf of her client," whereas *in behalf of* is supposed to mean "for the benefit of," as in "We raised money in behalf of the earthquake victims." But the two senses aren't that far apart, and people have been getting them mixed up since the late eighteenth century. In fact, when Weiner's predecessor James Murray was compiling the first edition of the *Oxford English Dictionary* in the 1880s, one of the people he cited for misusing *on behalf of* was Archbishop Richard Chevenix Trench, the great nineteenth-century scholar who was the *OED*'s spiritual father. In retrospect, it would have saved everybody a lot of trouble if Murray had just said, "Hey, if Trench can't keep this one straight, why don't we just bag it?"

There are a lot of pairs like this. Take the distinction between *masterful* and *masterly*. According to H. W. Fowler's classic *Modern English Usage*, one of them is supposed to mean "imperious or domineering" and the other is supposed to mean "with the skill of a master." I would be happy to remind you which is which, but I'm damned if I'm going to look the words up again. I figure that over the years they've already cost me a half-day out of my life.

Then there's the distinction between *each other* and *one another*. I was curious enough about this one to suggest a couple of years ago that we take it up with the usage panel of the *American Heritage Dictionary*, a group of about two hundred eminent writers and scholars that we poll every so often for their views on usage. About fifty percent of them said they used *each other* for two and *one another* for more than two. That's the rule you'll find in the traditional grammar books — you're supposed to say "The Smothers Brothers like each other, but the Three Stooges hate one another." But another thirty percent of the panelists had it the opposite way, and the rest of them just threw up their hands, which to tell the truth is what I would have done.

Actually that answer puts us in good company — it turns out that neither Samuel Johnson nor Noah Webster used *each other* and *one another* the way the rule says you're supposed to, either. And if Johnson and Webster couldn't keep this one straight, why can't we just agree to bag it? It's not like the difference between *disinterested* and *uninterested*, where you could argue that there's a risk of losing an important conceptual distinction. Even if I'm fuzzy on *each other* and *one another*, I'm still rock solid on the difference between two and three.

Still, those of us who write dictionaries and grammar books will have to keep dutifully setting down the rules. We know they have more to do with folklore than with fact — most of them were spun by grammarians out of whole cloth. And we're aware that nobody but purists will take them seriously. But people want to believe that wherever there are differences there must be distinctions, even if we're sometimes making them up as we go along.

Besides, there's a sense of satisfaction you can take in feeling that you're using words more precisely than other people, even if most of the time it's purely delusional. I'm a stickler on the difference between *partly* and *partially*, even though I know that writers from Jane Austen to James Joyce have paid no attention to it. It's the obeisance I pay to Mr. Painter, who explained it all one day in ninth-grade English when I was uncharacteristically in the mood to listen. And I've always taken a quiet pride in knowing the difference between *flotsam* and *jetsam* — the first is the wreckage that's floating on the water, the second is the stuff that's thrown overboard and washed ashore.

# Points in Your Favor  {2000}

I was telling a friend that I had gotten bogged down in the middle of the new Philip Roth novel *The Human Stain*, but that I always give Roth the benefit of the doubt. "What is it you see in him?" she asked. I said something about his intelligence and energy, and then, because that sounded kind of vague, I added, "Also, he's a great punctuator."

I realize that this puts me solidly in what you could think of as the Stradlaterian school of literary aesthetics. You remember Stradlater — Holden Caulfield's roommate at Pencey Prep. He asks Holden to write an English composition for him and then adds, "Just don't do it *too* good, is all . . . . Don't stick all the commas and stuff in the right place." And Holden says to the reader, "That's something that gives me a royal pain. I mean if you're good at writing compositions and somebody starts talking about commas."

It wasn't until many years after I read *The Catcher in the Rye* that it struck me how odd it was that Holden should assume that a concern for punctuation was a sign of the literary philistine and that the rest of us should so readily agree. But just imagine a composer getting huffy because someone suggests that the art of musical composition has something to do with putting rests in the right places. How did we get to the point where even our composition handbooks deal with punctuation under the heading of "mechanics"?

One reason why we moderns can take punctuation for granted is that we've shrunk the playing field to the point where the game doesn't seem to be much of a challenge anymore. Our sentences have gotten so short and so simple that punctuation seems to have a lot less work to do in holding them together. The tendency is easy to document. Not long ago the sociologist Todd Gitlin wrote a piece in *The Nation* reporting a study he'd done that showed that the length of the average sentence in novels on the *New York Times* bestseller list has decreased by more than twenty-five percent over the last sixty years, while the average number of punctuation marks per sentence has dropped by more than half.

But what should we make of this? Gitlin made his view clear when he called his article "The Dumbdown." But that doesn't necessarily follow. I don't know whether the average *New York Times* bestseller is dumber now than it was sixty years ago (though I for one would rather spend an evening with Harry Potter than with Pearl S. Buck). And in any case, the tendency isn't limited to popular books. To satisfy my curiosity, I made my own little study, but instead of looking at bestsellers I looked at the prestigious journal *Science*. The effect was the same — over the last hundred years, the average sentence has gotten markedly shorter and the number of punctuation marks per sentence has decreased by half. But I wouldn't describe this as a dumbdown — or at least *Science* hasn't become an easier read over the past century.

It's true that this isn't a universal phenomenon. For some reason, sentences in the *New York Times* have been pretty much the same length since the paper was founded in 1856, apart from an inexplicable dip in the 1950s. But in serious fiction the complex sentence has gotten pretty rare, particularly in the country of Melville and James. There are still a lot of British writers who are comfortable with classical rhythms — Salman Rushdie, certainly, and David Lodge, who turns this ornate syntax on and off at will. Or there's Martin Amis, whom reviewers are always complimenting for his well-turned sentences. But most modern American writers come to the dinner table holding only a comma and a dash to chop up their thoughts with. And that's not to mention writers like Raymond Carver, who seemed to think of sentences as a kind of finger food. I have the sense that Carver felt that every comma he had to stick in was a small defeat for prose minimalism.

When you mention simplified punctuation, people immediately start to talk about Hemingway. But there's nothing particularly Hemingwayesque about most modern prose fiction, even if it's held together with the same spare set of resources. You can do an astonishing range of voices with nothing but commas and dashes to work with: the witty turns of Lorrie Moore, the sprawling periods of David Foster Wallace, the jagged riffs of Don DeLillo. Or, for that matter, the deceptively colloquial ramblings of J. D. Salinger.

Still, I have a weakness for writers who build up their sentences with the full panoply of tools — writers who aren't diffident about occasionally dropping a semicolon into the middle of a parenthetical. That sort of punctuational virtuosity has a particular appeal in a writer like Roth, who brings it off in first-person narratives that don't evoke the august impersonal rhythms of nineteenth-century writers like George Eliot or Meredith. For all its complexity, it's a decidedly conversational and modern voice: you have the sense of listening to thoughts as they ramify, double back on themselves, break up, and come together again. They're like little prose arias, and sometimes I stop and go back to hear them over again.

The sentence is the expression of a complete thought. That's what Mr. Painter taught us back in the ninth grade, and I've been noodling it over ever since. You wouldn't think there could be so many different ways of putting thoughts together — so many right places to stick commas in, and so many wrong ones.

# Shall Game {2001}

To a linguist, the most bizarre single moment in the whole post-election brouhaha last fall came during the oral presentations to the Florida Supreme Court, as the parties argued over what the word *shall* meant in the statute that stipulates when the secretary of state is supposed to certify the vote. Was the outcome of an American presidential election really going to depend on the interpretation of a word that no American since Henry James has known how to use properly?

*Shall* is the flower of what H. W. Fowler called "the English of the English." But it never took root in American soil outside of the stony fields of old New England. It's certainly not the kind of linguistic fillip you can pick up in the course of a junior year abroad. As the nineteenth-century Bostonian Richard Grant White put it, the distinction between *shall* and *will* is too subtle for "persons who have not had the advantage of early intercourse with educated English people. I mean English in blood and breeding . . . ."

Indeed, the rules for using *shall* and *will* are as thorny and tangled as an English bramble. Fowler devoted seven columns to his entry on *shall* (a model of conciseness when you compare it to the forty-three columns on *shall* and *will* in the *Oxford English Dictionary*). Even so, he doubted whether his explanation of the distinction would be of much use to anyone who hadn't had the advantages of a southern English upbringing; as he said, "Those who are not to the manner born can hardly acquire it."

Anyone who has wrestled with the rules will readily agree. For one thing, the meanings of *shall* and *will* change according to the subject. *You shall* or *he shall* expresses an obligation or makes a promise; *you will* or *he will* makes a simple prediction or a statement of desire. When an Englishman tells you, "You shall have your money," he means that he is going to pay you; when he says, "You will have your money," you can whistle for it. But in the first person the meanings are reversed: here it's *I shall* that makes the prediction, and *I will* that expresses resolution or intention. The difference is summed up in an old story about the Frenchman who is foundering in the waves off Brighton and yells, "I will drown and no one shall save me" — so nobody does.

We Americans, too, can have trouble keeping our heads above water when we extend our use of *shall* beyond those first-person-plural questions like "Shall we?" General MacArthur got it backwards when he announced his intention to recapture the Philippines by saying, "I shall return." By Fowler's lights, that's the sort of thing you say when you're going out for a quart of milk.

But then, why would any self-respecting American want to touch this word with a bargepole? When I hear an American reaching for a *shall*, I recall the flap when a protocol officer in Reagan's White House was photographed curtseying to Queen Elizabeth. As one critic remarked, "Didn't we fight a war about that?" And it's hard to escape the feeling that Americans who use the word are not entirely trustworthy — as James Thurber wrote, "Men who use *shall* west of the Appalachians are the kind who twirl canes and eat ladyfingers."

In fact, the word *shall* is pretty shifty in its own right. When I ask lawyers why they are so attached to the word they usually tell me what their law school professors told them, that *shall* somehow avoids the ambiguities and imprecisions of ordinary English speech. But that's hardly the impression I get when I look up *shall* in the fourth edition of *Black's Law Dictionary*, which I bought at a garage sale some years ago. It's true that *Black's* says that *shall* is "generally imperative or mandatory" when it's used in contracts or statutes. But it goes on to say that *shall* "may be construed as merely permissive or directory," and it adds that the word often implies "an element of futurity." In short, *shall* means *must,* except for when it means *may* or *should* or *will.* (And except for when it doesn't mean any of those. "This Act shall be known as the Penal Code of California" — does that mean I could get in trouble if I call it something else?)

In Australia, where the movement to reform legal language has gained a lot of ground, one state has actually banned the use of the word *shall* from legislation as a way of expressing obligation, insisting that drafters use *must* instead. It's an eminently sensible move. Why would we want a word as slippery as *shall* determining the filing date for tax returns, much less the selection of a president?

But it's hard to imagine the American legal establishment tossing *shall* over the side. Maybe it's the symbolic value of the word — as the legal scholar Frederick Bowers puts it, *shall* is a kind of totem that conjures up the flavor of the law. Or maybe it's the way *shall* tends to infuse a document with the smell of old port and oak paneling. That has to be an appealing feature to a profession whose practitioners are rolling into the twenty-first century with the title *Esq.* still appended to their names.

# Literacy Literacy   {2001}

The Bushes are back, bringing literacy with them. I don't mean to suggest that the Clinton administration in any way neglected the issue, but the Bushes have made it a family cause, and we'll doubtless be hearing the word *literacy* a lot more often. It's hard to take exception with that concern. For the last hundred fifty years or so, Americans have regarded literacy as an absolute public good, which is probably why we keep broadening its tent.

The word *literate* has been around since the Renaissance as a way of describing someone with a liberal education — in the eighteenth century, Lord Chesterfield defined *illiterate* as "a man who is ignorant of [Greek and Latin]." But these were recondite words until the late nineteenth century, when Americans started to use them to classify people according to whether they could read and write. That was the moment when literacy became a civic virtue, the key to creating the responsible public that a democracy seemed to require. As one reformer put it, universal education was "the lever that will elevate the social state of the poor — assimilating them in habits, thoughts, and feelings to the rich and the educated." It was the great age of the American public library movement, as idealistic librarians went forth to serve as "apostles of culture," as one historian described them. And from then on, people have considered literacy rates the best indicators of a nation's social development.

Since that period, *literacy* and *illiteracy* have led double lives in English: they refer both to basic skills and to broader cultural and intellectual achievements, to the point where the vast majority of people count as literate by one standard and illiterate by some other. And more recently, Americans have been broadening the notion of literacy still further to cover skills and knowledge that don't seem to have any immediate connection to basic reading and writing. The phrases "media literacy" and "economic literacy" first appeared about fifty or sixty years ago, and in the following decades people began to talk about geographical literacy, scientific literacy, computer literacy, and mathematical literacy, which is sometimes described as numeracy. By 1987, the critic E. D. Hirsch could coin the term "cultural literacy" to cover all of the information that Americans need to know in order to function as informed citizens, which he has conveniently summarized in lists and dictionaries: who were the Rough Riders, what was the Stamp Act, where is Stuttgart, when was the Thirty Years' War? Shortly after that, William Bennett started using "moral literacy" for the ethical principles that all children ought to be taught — values they would presumably extract from the uplifting tales in Bennett's *Book of Virtues*.

I don't know of any other language that has a single word that covers this range of territory. When the French, Italians, or Portuguese want to talk about the ability to read and write, they use terms based on the word *alphabet*. Someone who doesn't have those skills is called analphabetic, literacy rates are called alphabetization rates, and so forth. But when it comes to describing the other kinds of knowledge that Americans call literacies of one kind or another, Europeans use other words, like "learning" or "culture." The phrase *computer literacy* translates into Italian as *la cultura del computer*. And if you wanted to talk about cultural literacy, you'd have to say something like *la cultura della cultura*, though that expression doesn't make much sense to Italians.

Of course there are a number of words in English that don't have exact translations in other languages — *smug*, for example, or *empowerment*. But when that happens, it's a good bet there's some sleight of hand going on. The fact is that there's nothing natural or obvious about using the same word to describe the basic ability to read and write and the general knowledge and values that we want our citizens to have.

In part, all this talk of literacies reflects the skittishness that Americans have about using the word *culture* as a positive term. We have no problem using the word to describe the traditions and mores of particular groups and communities, like when we talk about corporate culture, hip-hop culture, or RV culture. And there's a growing tendency to use the phrase "the culture" to refer to the custard of values and prejudices that we're all swimming around in. (As Cullen Murphy has pointed out, we often use that phrase when we want to let ourselves off the hook for some disturbing social trend, as in "The culture normalizes sexual harassment.")

But we're uncomfortable about using the bare noun *culture* all by itself, particularly when it's invested with positive associations. A phrase like "a person of culture" has an elitist, PBS ring to it. And no one would get very far trying to argue that the schools are failing in their duty to turn out cultivated citizens. That might be a perfectly natural thing to say in French, but in American English the adjective *cultivated* is reserved for seniors who are describing themselves in a personal ad.

Since the nineteenth century the word *literacy* has been the American way of getting culture in through the back door of the schoolroom. *Literacy* strips culture of its connotations of class and refinement and turns it into a civic duty and a subject matter, something you can objectify and quantify. At that point it becomes natural to start compiling lists of all the things that people ought to know, particularly given the modern American passion for measurement—and for lists, for that matter. If learning about citizenship or morality is the same sort of thing as learning to write and read, then we ought to be able to set down the subject in a dictionary, the same way we do with words and spellings. Of course, as soon as anybody publishes one of these lists, people start to quibble with its contents — why list Horace Greeley and not Marcus Garvey? But that's how people always greet the appearance of a new dictionary. And as soon as we start arguing over which items to include, we validate the appropriateness of treating culture as a lexicographical exercise in the first place — now we're only haggling.

There has always been an element of social control in the importance Americans attach to literacy. The nineteenth-century founders of the public library movement believed that universal literacy was the best way of inoculating the poor against radical influences — public libraries, as one supporter said, would ensure "the deliverance of the people from the wiles of the rhetorician and stump orator." But there was also a sincere hope that once people learned to read and write they'd be exposed to a world of experience where everything wasn't codified in advance. That's a notion that can be hard to discern in the way we use *literacy* now, where we make the mastery of basic reading and writing the model for everything that we want to go on in the classroom. It runs the risk of reducing the whole of education to a spelling bee.

# technical terms

# The Dactyls of October  {1995}

I've been looking at these new magazines, like *Wired* and *Mondo 2000*. Cyberzines, they call themselves, the *Vanity Fair* and *Interview* of the information age. As best I can figure, the information age runs from eighteen to twenty-five; that's doubtless why the magazines have an MTV look to them, with jazzy fonts on colored backgrounds, text running over the pictures. It's all very engaging, but a little hard to read for someone of my decade and diopter. I find myself yearning for the austere simplicity of the black-and-white screen on my antique Mac. But maybe that's the point of these magazines, to drive us all online. Cyberquislings, subverting print culture from within.

The magazines are strewn with evocations of the 60s, with all its talk of revolution — how the technology is going to lead to universal empowerment and the end of hierarchy. You might think nothing had changed in the last thirty years, except that now the relevant technology is software engineering instead of pharmacology. It's not surprising to find Timothy Leary on the editorial board of *Mondo 2000*, having decided to drop in again now that things are once more getting interesting.

But the language of the age has nothing to do with the 60s. It's cyberspeak, all those compounds patched together from the truncated syllables of other words, always in the same rhythm: *cyberspace, Internet, Ethernet, hypertext, middleware, ubicomp, nanotech, infobahn.* You think of the fighter planes in the old comic strips: *pock*eta, *pock*eta, *pock*eta, *pock*eta. I have heard the future, and it speaks in dactyls. It's a rhythm we've heard before, but not at Woodstock. This is the music of October 1917. It's the way the Bolsheviks consolidated their words, as ruthlessly as they consolidated everything else: *Comintern, agitprop,*

*Komsomol, Komkultur, Sovnarkom.* The words had a willful ugliness, as George Orwell put it, as if to signal a break with bourgeois aesthetics. It was the language of technological efficiency, literally telegraphic, the clipped syntax required for communication by wire.

The resemblances to cyberspeak are more than accidental. For one thing, current computers constrain the shape of words in some of the same ways that the telegraph did. There are the programming languages that won't accept expressions with extra spaces in them and the operating systems that won't let you use more than eight letters for a filename, so that all your files wind up with titles like TaxInfo.txt. And when cyberspeak picks up the pattern, it's as if to say, This is how we have to talk when we let machines be a party in the conversation.

There are indirect historical connections as well. The terminology of Soviet Communism was the model for Orwell's Newspeak — words like *doublethink* and *Minipax*, not to mention the name *Newspeak* itself. And that in turn was the idiom that William Gibson transformed to make the language of cyberpunk, which took newspeak from gray to noir. It was Gibson who coined *cyberspace*. It's the sort of word that Big Brother would have used if he'd been a radio evangelist in Raymond Chandler's L.A.

Of course the new cyberspeak doesn't have the dark, oppressive overtones of its predecessors. It's upbeat and hopeful. But there was a brief moment when the Russian Revolution was light and gay, too. It was the time of the Constructivist avant-garde, with their collectives, their paeans to bridges and machines, their new forms of theater — not to mention the typographical experiments that are the direct progenitors of the graphics in *Wired* and the rest.

I'll grant you that the comparison has its limits. The digital revolution has produced some interesting creative works, but it has yet to turn out a Malevitch or a Mayakovsky. For that matter, we should feel a little embarrassed about calling this a revolution at all, at least by contrast with what happened in October 1917. It's more like a virtual revolution, where everybody gets to lead the charge on the Winter Palace and nobody actually has to be carried off on a litter. Still, it's a great time to be young and online, and perhaps November will come in a little milder this time around, with Big Brother replaced by a cheery little soul named Bob.

# Virtual Rialto {1995}

**H**ave you seen these new IBM ads with the "global village" theme, about how technology makes Americans
of us all? There are the two French gaffers walking along
the Seine and talking about disk drives while accordions
play in the background. The subtitles have one of them saying, "My hard drive's maxed out," and the other responding
with something that's translated as "Bummer!" Or there's
the clutch of Czech nuns talking about operating systems as
the mother superior says, "I'm dying to surf the Internet."
Of course — they wish they all could be California girls.

The Romans used to refer to the Mediterranean as *Mare
Nostrum*, "our sea," and Americans tend to think of the electronic world in the same way, invoking all the stock American
images of wide-open spaces. You're a Net surfer, you're a cow-
boy on the electronic frontier. You're standing on the bridge of
your own private *Enterprise* about to boldly go where no one
has gone before. Or you're a cyber-Kerouac cruising the information highway with the top down and the virtual wind in
your hair.

The thing of it is that when you get on the Net it really
doesn't feel much like any of these. It's hard to imagine anything that's less like the ocean, the prairie, the cosmos, or the
highway. There are no vistas here, no expanses stretching out
endlessly ahead of you. And there's no frontier, no place to go
out there that someone else hasn't gone before. The Net has
nothing to do with the wide-open spaces of the New World, and
everything to do with the cramped, crooked cities of the Old.
It's urban, close, interior. If you are looking for a good metaphor
for the Internet, in fact, go to Venice in February. You thread
your way down foggy streets and over bridges till you lose all

sense of compass direction, and then all of a sudden you break into some glorious piazza. The rusty gate on the alley over there might open into a lush garden, and behind that might be a palazzo with long enfilades of rooms and galleries, but you can't see anything from the street. It's a place you get to know as an accumulation of paths and hidden passages, the way a woodsman knows the forest. A Venetian friend told me once that she knows no more pathetic sight than watching one of her neighbors trying to give some help to a tourist who holds out a map and asks how to get to the San Rocco. We Venetians have no idea how to read a map of our city, she said, all we know is how to get from A to B without getting our feet wet.

That's perfect for the Internet: the virtual Rialto. Except that Venice is too permanent — you come back after fifty years and everything's right where it was when you left. Whereas on the Internet addresses and connections change daily. Maybe we want to think of it as the Venice that Italo Calvino might have invented as one of his invisible cities, a fantastic place where houses move overnight from one quarter to another, where bridges disappear and canals reroute themselves with no warning. Perhaps it's like the Moroccan soukh in another of those IBM ads, a warren of stalls that open and close unaccountably. Or maybe the model isn't an Old World city at all, but one of those shantytowns that spring up overnight on the outskirts of Latin American cities — the *barriadas* of Lima, the *favelas* of Rio. The one sure thing is that it's nothing like Wyoming or the coast of southern California. It isn't even much like a Houston shopping mall, with its long sight lines and its standardized chain-store interface. It's a more exotic locale for us than for the rest of the world, and there is always the possibility that we will be the ones who feel like tourists there.

# The Talking Gambit    {1997}

**I**t's only human to hate to lose, so it isn't surprising that people have come up with a slew of excuses and explanations for Deep Blue's victory over Garry Kasparov last weekend. The machine wasn't really thinking, they say, as if that was a kind of cheating. Or they say the outcome would have been different if Kasparov had had more time to rest between games or if he'd gotten a look at Deep Blue's previous play before the match. But there was no way to make this a perfectly fair fight. It's like staging a boxing match between Mike Tyson and a kangaroo — there wouldn't be any ring size that would work equally well for both competitors. However you try to explain it away, it was still a great moment in the history of the computer, and a poetic comeuppance for all those philosophers and pundits who were saying twenty years ago that a computer would never be able to beat a human chess master.

But let's not get apocalyptic about this. What the match proved in the end, after all, was only that a computer that had been training with a grandmaster could beat a grandmaster who had been training with a computer. And there was never that much difference between those parties to begin with. In the vast landscape of the human condition, the chess players and the computer programmers live in pretty much the same neighborhood, and what's more, it's something of a gated community. If the ability to write code in C or to appreciate the subtleties of the Sicilian Defense were emblematic of humanity, most of us would be disqualified at the outset. And maybe Deep Blue's victory will help everybody focus on the things that really make our species special — not the recondite mental gymnastics of tournament chess, but the ordinary things we take for granted, like talking.

Every few months, it seems, some software developer announces a breakthrough program that has licked some basic linguistic capability — it can converse in ordinary language, or translate French into English, or understand queries like "Where is Joey Buttafuoco from?" People buy the story hook, line, and sinker and proceed to drive up the stock price for a couple of months until the program turns out to be a collection of hacks like all the others. It's true that researchers have made impressive progress in these areas, but computers are not even close to being able to deal with language in a naturalistic way. Put it this way: if machines could play games no better than they could understand and produce human language, they'd have a hard time keeping up with an eight-year-old at tick-tack-toe.

Why is language so hard? For one thing, the rules are extraordinarily complicated; they bear the same relation to chess as the federal tax code does to the rules of a magazine sweepstakes. Then too, the use of language doesn't stand on its own; it rests on a rich background of knowledge of the world. The other day I heard someone whistling "Blowin' in the Wind" and somebody else said, "You know, he's got a new album out." Think what I had to know to figure out who that pronoun *he* referred to.

One other point that we tend to lose sight of is that language isn't just a question of brains, but of bodies. I don't know if a computer could think, or whether it could be conscious; it's hard even to make sense of those notions, much less prove them one way or the other. What's certain is that a computer will never understand an ordinary human word like *rue*. You might teach it to realize that it had made a mistaken move in chess —

though that's hard by itself — and maybe you could even cause it to dwell on the fact excessively. But a machine can't comprehend the way Kasparov must have felt when he mixed up the order of the opening moves in the fifth game — that sudden rush of shit to the heart.

Will computers ever be able to converse the way we do? The Deep Blue episode should warn us off making categorical predictions, but it's a safe bet that nobody alive today will be a party to the conversation. The one thing that's absolutely certain is that computers will never do language *better* than we do — no more than they'll ever be better at singing saloon ballads. These are our games, and you have to play them by our standards. I'll grant you that Kasparov is a great phenomenon, but *Newsweek* was wrong to describe him as the hope of humanity. That honor belongs to the kibitzers at ringside.

# Lost in Space   {1997}

Just a few years ago, the Internet was going to be an unmixed blessing: we were going to tear down the walls of the libraries and just let all that information float free in space, where anyone could have access to it. As one visionary put it: "Cyberspace: A world in which the global traffic of knowledge, secrets, measurements, indicators, entertainments . . . takes on form: sights, sounds, presences never seen on the surface of the earth blossoming in a vast electronic night." That was written back in 1991, and you can tell. The problem isn't that the writer got the Internet wrong. "The global traffic of knowledge, secrets, measurements, indicators, entertainments" — that's the World Wide Web to a T. But the unbridled enthusiasm for the new realm has waned decidedly as people have started to spend time in it. That vast electronic night isn't quite so romantic when you're stumbling around trying to find your slippers amongst all the other junk on the floor.

It's true that a lot of this comes with the territory. All the misinformation, the vanity pages, the porn, the infomercials — well, what did we expect? When you tear down the walls of the library, you shouldn't be surprised to find all the street people camped out in the reading room. And users are only just beginning to learn what library cataloguers have known for a long time — just how hard it is to find your way around when you have only words to do your bidding.

You can get a graphic sense of the confusion when you log on to a website called Voyeur, which is provided by the people who run the Magellan Internet search service. Every fifteen seconds or so the Voyeur site throws up a dozen randomly selected strings of search words that people have typed into the search engine. They roll out in a jumble: cherubim... fixed income derivatives... up skirt white panties... aerosmith pics ... do skunks turn white in the winter... crack... Eisenhower High School, 1981... Pamela Anderson's feet... what would Jesus have done?

What a bunch! It's like overhearing the babble of voices around a subway newsstand as you rush to catch your train, except that few of these queries are designed to get the right pages off the rack. I don't know what was in the mind of the person who typed in the word *crack*, for example, which pulled down an assortment that included porn sites, drug information, the descramblers that hackers call cracks, and a technical report on stress in metals. I'm pretty sure, though, that the requester was shortly complaining about what a mess the Internet is.

The only people who seem exempt from this problem are the porn seekers. Their search strings are as inept as any others: "dogs getting it," "shaven sluts," "schoolgirls," or the plaintive one-word query "nookie." But it turns out that most of those lame efforts hit their mark quite well — this thanks to the accommodating porn providers, who know how the search engines work and lade their sites with just about every word and expression that someone might enter in the hope of reaching them: there was one I saw that listed five different spellings for *fellatio*. In fact the porn consumers must be about the only users of the web who don't have to disabuse themselves of the impression that the search engines can read their minds. But then, theirs are pretty easy minds to read.

But what about the rest of us, whose objectives may be a little more difficult to grasp? The visionaries keep telling us that help is just around the corner in the form of intelligent agents, systems that will figure out our interests and tastes and take us unerringly to exactly the information we are looking for. But it's clear that the people who glibly describe these things haven't ever watched a flesh-and-blood librarian manage to extract a sense from the incoherent mumbles of the customers who present themselves at the reference desk. It's true there will be tools to make navigating the Net a lot easier, but in the end, users are going to have to spend a lot of time learning to meet the technology halfway, the way we spend a couple of years of junior high school learning how to look up words in the dictionary. Or maybe it's just a matter of doing the old lessons right. That's one thing the visionaries didn't realize about cyberspace: spelling counts.

# A Wink Is As Good As a Nod   {1997}

**M**ichael Kinsley is the latest high-profile journalist to make the shift from print to pixels, as the editor of Microsoft's new online magazine *Slate*. But he doesn't believe that the fundamental differences between the two media are that pronounced; *Slate*, he writes, "won't scream 'cyberspace,' but just suggest it with a wink." I surmise that Kinsley was talking about winking in a purely metaphorical way, but in electronic discourse the winks are often a bit more literal, when they come in the form of a smiley — a string of punctuation marks suggesting a facial expression laid on its side. You can end your sentence with :-) to indicate a smile, with ;-) to indicate a wink, or with :-( to suggest a frown of unhappiness or displeasure. Imaginative e-writers have come up with hundreds of these things, expressions that signal sourness, sleepiness, wryness, surprise, alarm, and so on. Sometimes they're called emoticons, a word that blends *emotion* and *icon*. (It deserves to die horribly in a head-on collision with *infotainment*.)

In its own small way, the smiley is as significant a sign of the revolutionary implications of digital media as anything else I can think of. After all, the repertory of Western punctuation has been pretty much fixed since the sixteenth century — a measly half-dozen or so marks to render all the tones and nuances that the human voice is capable of. Until now, that is, when their expressive power is augmented so dramatically that it's like moving from a quill pen to a high-powered workstation.

It's a pity earlier writers didn't have these devices at their disposal. The frownie would have been useful to Kafka in "The Metamorphosis":

Gregor Samsa awoke one morning to find himself transformed into a monstrous insect :-(

Proust could have used a yawnie to emphasize the first sentence
of *Remembrance of Things Past*:

For a long time, I went to bed early |-O

And with Jane Austen, of course, it would have been winkies all
the way down:

It is a truth universally acknowledged, that a single man in
possession of a good fortune must be in want of a wife ;-)

I can hear you Janeites getting shirty: surely *she* would never
have stooped to such a device. Well, maybe not, so long as she
was sending her words in print to an anonymous audience. But
I suspect she would have given serious consideration to the expedient if she were planning to send the text electronically to a
list like rec.fiction, if only to spare herself the flames that would
otherwise have come searing back over the Net.

To: Jane@chawton.uk
From: sparky123@aol.com
Subject: Universally Acknowledged . . . NOT!

Get real, Jane! "A truth universally acknowledged"? Have
you done a poll on the subject? >:-<

Like most traditionalists, I've resisted using smileys in my e-
mail. It feels too much like tipping my hand: I flatter myself
that I can convey my tone without any need of a key signature.
But it has occurred to me that I may be denying myself a useful
device out of a weakness for the same fond illusion that the

inventors of the smiley were prey to, the notion that any mere marks can pin down the meaning of your words in an unambiguous way. Irony is a pervasive sensibility, which has a way of washing over any sea walls we put in its path. The other day I got a message from a friend who congratulated me in fulsome terms for having slipped out of a particularly disagreeable obligation. It had a winkie tacked to the end of it, but I could tell he meant that ironically, too.

# How the Web Was Won   {1998}

**P**eople don't always get new technologies right when they first appear. You can tell from the names they tack on to them. *Railroad,* for example, which wound up being not much of a road at all. Or *radio,* which began as a shortened form of *radiotelegraphy* back in the days when everyone thought the medium would be most useful for ship-to-shore communications.

I have the sense that *cyberspace* will have the same quaint connotations a couple of generations from now. Partly it's that prefix *cyber–*. It was all the rage a few years ago, but now it seems to be yielding to the prefix *e–*, which has spread from *e-mail* to a host of names like *e-commerce, e-cash, e-shopping,* and so on. One advantage of the *e–* prefix is that it's usually written lowercase, even in proper names. That fits nicely with the current style of corporate nomenclature — it's a useful way of suggesting that your company is cutting-edge, by showing that you're not trammeled by the orthographic conventions of the old wave. When I squint at a list of new stock offerings, it looks something like the table of contents of a collection of modernist poetry, one where e. e. cummings is given especial pride of place.

Mostly, though, the rise of *e–* signals a change in the way people are thinking about the medium. *Cyber–* invokes the romance of the Internet. The prefix actually comes from the Greek root for "government," but that's hard to hear in the way people use it to evoke a sense of the Internet as an open range. The *e–* prefix came into its own when the land rush began and everybody started staking out a little piece of the territory and branding everything they could get their iron on. *E-commerce, e-cash, e-trade* — those are the words you hear when you hang out around neighborhoods like South Park in San Francisco, where five thousand twenty-somethings are milling around waving business plans for companies to sell nail polish on the web.

It's true that *cyber–* is still being used, particularly when people want to avoid the narrowly commercial implications of *e–*. If you do a search on the web you'll find words like *cyber-pet*, *cyber-romance*, *cyberchurch*, and *cyber-Uzbekistan*. And of course people still talk about cybersex. I don't know exactly what e-sex would be, but I have the feeling it would show up on my Visa bill.

Still, it's clear that *cyber–* is losing ground to *e–* as the web becomes more commercialized and densely populated. The web may still be a place, but it doesn't feel much like the wide-open spaces these days. Now the talk is all of "niches" and "portals," the latter a word that has become wildly popular in the last year or so. At first it was used just for the search engines and web indexes like Infoseek and Yahoo!, which were trying to grab a spot as everybody's entry point to the Internet. Now you hear it used for any site that tries to provide links to a particular type of product or service. Firms are angling to become the gift portal, the travel portal, the real estate portal, and so on. In the tempestuous climate of e-business, the new rule seems to be "any portal in a storm."

Not all of the portal companies are happy about the word. It suggests that people might log on to them and then go somewhere else, whereas the companies are trying to provide a range of services that make it unnecessary for anyone to leave their site. Or if you are bold enough to venture out on the web on your own, they want you to think of their site as a comforting place you can come back to if you get lost or in trouble. In an interview in the *Wall Street Journal*, the CEO of Lycos suggests that he'd like their site to be thought of as a "hub." I have my doubts about that one: it makes me think of spending two and a half hours on the ground at the Denver or Cincinnati airport thumbing through copies of *Savvy* and *Trailer Life*. Reading dumb stuff while you wait for your connection — that probably isn't a feature that the search sites want to draw their customers' attention to.

# The Software We Deserve   {1998}

**T**o the list of crimes and derelictions that Bill Gates has been charged with, we can now add the murder of the English language. At least that's the opinion of the writer Ralph Schoenstein, in a recent op-ed piece in the *New York Times* on the Microsoft Word grammar checker. Schoenstein complains that the checker doesn't flag the simplest errors. It doesn't protest when you modify absolute terms like *unique*, as in "She was a most unique woman." It makes no objection when you fail to use the subjunctive in a sentence like "If I was a player, I would go." And so on for dozens of other traditional rules of usage.

Actually the only mystery here is why anyone would expect grammar checkers to work as well as spell checkers. Maybe people have just been so snowed by technohype that they expect computers to be able to do anything — if they can beat a grandmaster at chess, why can't they edit a simple freshman composition? But copy-editing calls for a lot more discrimination than playing chess, and discrimination isn't computers' long suit. You might want your checker to flag "His rugs are most unique," on the grounds that either something is unique or it isn't. But you'd want it to accept "Most unique rugs command high prices," or, for that matter, "His rugs are almost unique." Spotting those distinctions is a lot harder than figuring out if someone has spelled *weird* with *ei* or *ie*. When you think about what's involved in the process, in fact, it's impressive that the checkers can accomplish even simple things like spotting the subject-verb agreement error in the sentence "The boy have left."

The real problem with grammar checkers isn't that they fail to catch so many obvious problems, it's that they're built to spot so many bogus ones. As time goes by they seem to pander more and more to all the infantile schoolroom prejudices that people have about usage. Back in the days when checkers were sold as standalone software, I talked to a woman who was in charge of checker development at a small software house. When she started out, she said, she was full of high hopes about bringing grammatical uplift to the masses. It's certainly an alluring prospect, the idea that writers might have a grammatical angel hovering permanently at their shoulders. But when she started talking to the sales people she was quickly disabused. "How come our checker doesn't flag split infinitives?" they'd ask her, and she'd say, "Oh, that's just a stupid superstition." And they'd answer, "Well, it may be stupid, but the other checkers have it, and they're using it as a selling point against ours." So of course in went the split infinitive, along with all the other schoolroom fetishes that have been giving grammar a bad name for centuries — don't end a sentence with a preposition, don't begin a sentence with *and* or *but*, and of course avoid the passive. After a while that angel over your shoulder starts to sound less like H. W. Fowler than like Richard Simmons.

You can't blame the computer for this dumbing down — the trivialization of usage was accelerating well before Bill Gates was graduated from what used to be called grammar school. You can see it in the newspaper language columns, the publishing houses that have taken to firing their copy editors to save money, or the textbooks that list all of these rules under the heading "sentence mechanics." And you can see it in the reverence that people accord to Strunk and White's little book, *The Elements of Style*, which has done more than anything else to persuade people that the whole subject of usage can be reduced to a few pithy maxims that even a computer could understand.

In the end, it may well be that grammar checkers will seal

the fate of usage. Writing is like most of the other tasks we perform by means of the computer, from web searching to talking to voice recognition software: after a while we learn to accommodate ourselves to the limits of the technology. In every relationship, after all, somebody has to be the adaptable one. If computers can't distinguish between the passive sentences that make sense and the ones that don't, we'll spare ourselves a lot of problems by avoiding the whole construction. It won't be Bill Gates's fault, though. An age gets the software it deserves.

# Have It My Way {1998}

**E**very once in a while my eight-year-old daughter comes up to me when I'm working and puts her arm around me in a transparently insincere display of affection, then walks away giggling. As soon as she's gone, I pat my hand around on my back to find a Post-it that says something like "I'm a knucklehead." You'd think that pronoun *I* wouldn't mean anything if I didn't put it there myself, but somehow I'm implicit in the utterance. She has visited a small indignity on me, and we both know it.

This is about the most powerful magic you can work with writing, putting a first-person pronoun into somebody else's mouth. It was probably no more than a couple of weeks after the invention of cuneiform in Sumer five millennia ago that some scribe had the idea of pressing the characters for "Kick me" into a clay tablet and fastening it to the back of the robes of a passing priest.

But the game didn't really come into its own until recent times, as writing spread to every aspect of our lives. Buttons, T-shirts, bumper stickers, magazine inserts, credit agreements — all of them are full of first-person pronouns that other people have obligingly fashioned for our use. "I ♥ SF." "My grandmother went to Hawaii and all I got was this lousy T-shirt." "Bill me now." Most of these we tack on more or less willingly, but some of them just come with the job. You have to feel sympathy for those drivers who roll around all day in company vans with stickers on the bumpers that say, "How am I driving? Call 555-1234." It's just a sophisticated version of the "Kick me" game, though I suspect the trucking companies justify it by saying that they want the drivers to feel a sense of ownership about their turn signals.

The designers of new technologies were quick to catch on to this maneuver. You log in and there's a page labeled "My Yahoo!" or "My Excite" where you can set your own interest profile. I turn on my PC and I see a little icon on the Windows desktop that's labeled "My Computer," Microsoft's way of providing me with a proprietary feeling about my file directories. In a way this is the biggest breakthrough in pronoun control since Sumer. It isn't like the "How am I driving?" bumper sticker, where the company that owns the truck is talking through the driver's voice to the other people on the road. Here you have Microsoft or Yahoo! supplying both ends of the conversation, referring to the user with "my" at the same time they're referring to themselves with "we." It's like watching a video game in demo mode, where the software makes all your moves for you.

That's what a lot of interactivity seems to come down to, online or off. It's the same story whether you're consulting a webpage, filling out a customer satisfaction survey, or trying to find out your Visa balance over a telephone voice menu. In the end the bandwidth is always asymmetric: you upload clicks and download pages. The first-person pronouns may give the illusion of conversation, but people are pretty jaded by now — they've been onto this game since they were eight.

# The Writing on the Walls  {1999}

The House of Representatives has just passed its own version of the crime bill, which includes a provision that gives states the right to post the Ten Commandments in the schools. According to Representative Bob Barr, a Georgia Republican, this might well have prevented the Littleton slayings. I doubt that he would have made the same claim for a proposal to send the Commandments around in an email chain letter or print them in the front of the yearbook. It's an impressive indication of the faith we still invest occasionally in the power of epigraphic writing — that is, writing on walls and other public places. And it's all the more striking when you think what low esteem we have for this kind of writing in other situations. If there's a single architectural motto that characterizes the modern age, it would be "Post No Bills." We restrict billboards and deplore graffiti, and if we must have signs over stores or on buildings, we pass ordinances to ensure that they are as unobtrusive as possible. A couple of weeks ago I picked up a lavish picture book about Los Angeles published by the Chamber of Commerce and was astonished to find that it didn't contain a single picture of a billboard or electric sign; as far as the civic leaders are concerned, apparently, the lively clash of public messages on Pico Boulevard is no more fit for reproduction than the city's red-light district.

For our age, it's the writing we find in the private space between the covers of a book that does most of the cultural heavy lifting. But as the historian Armando Petrucci has noted, this is a relatively recent notion. In classical Rome, most of the important writing was found in public spaces. The only part of this writing that survives today, of course, is the inscriptions on monuments and public buildings. But visitors to any city in the Roman Empire in the first century B.C. would have seen writing wherever they looked — carved into wooden tablets hung from doorways, traced on white squares, scrawled or scratched on the surfaces of walls, columns, and streets.

This tradition of public writing pretty much vanished in the Middle Ages, along with the conception of public life itself, but it re-emerged in the neoclassical façades of the Renaissance. And when the printed book first appeared, printers naturally took those forms of writing as their models. They mimicked the monumental typefaces and included frontispieces that inscribed the titles of the books on engravings of classical structures, as if the books themselves were miniature public monuments.

By the eighteenth century, though, the culture of the book had already triumphed, to the point where architectural monuments were beginning to inscribe their writing on carved books, in a reversal of the process. Epigraphy in all its forms had been consigned to largely commercial or practical roles — shop signs, official announcements, or penny journalism. These were not negligible functions — the historian David Henkin has pointed out just how central the experience of wall writing was in the shaping of the American city. But with a few exceptions, like the graphical experiments of artists like the Russian Futurists or Jenny Holzer, epigraphy plays a decidedly minor role in what we like to describe as "print culture."

For better or worse, people tend to think of the computer and the web as the successor to the book as a means of cultural expression. That's what leads to these endless discussions of what you want to be playing with in your lap when you go to bed at night. The fact is, though, that the book is a poor model for what happens on the screen. We talk about webpages, for example, but really the things that come up in your browser aren't like pages at all — they go rolling off the screen, and you can't get your thumb and forefinger around them. And it's even worse when people try to make web documents resemble books; you have the feeling that you're looking at a volume in a glass case.

On the other hand, computers are an ideal medium for making models of buildings — you can zoom in and out or wander effortlessly from room to room and façade to façade, all of this with the added advantage of being able to send the whole edifice out over a wire. It makes you wonder what Michelangelo or Pirro Ligorio could have done with wall writing if only they'd had a graphics card on their PCs.

The web feels more like a public space than like a library of books. That's implicit in the way we talk about building sites and portals that people can go to. The only difference is that on the web the common point is the one you start off at, rather than where you wind up. (A good motto for the portal companies would be "All Roads Lead from Rome.") A few years ago I edited a book on new technologies called *The Future of the Book*. If I had it to do over again, I'd call it *The Future of Writing*.

# Its Own Reward   {2000}

*Virtual* has been doing solid journeyman work in English since Chaucer's time. It's related to *virtue*, but not in the William Bennett sense of the word; it's derived from the old use of *virtue* to mean "essence" or "capability," a sense that still survives in the phrase "in virtue of." So *virtual* means "in essence if not in fact" or "for all practical purposes," as when you say that So-and-So ruled as a virtual king.

*Virtual*'s recent run started when engineers found it a useful term to describe the computer's ability to create simulations. "Virtual memory" is a way of faking RAM that you don't actually have, and a "virtual machine" is the kind of system that lets your Macintosh pretend it's a PC or vice versa. Those technical usages didn't really stretch the original meaning of the word. It was in the late 1980s that the adjective began to capture the public imagination, with the coining of the term *virtual reality* to describe systems that simulate various kinds of sensory experience. The basic technology may have been old hat, as such things go — NASA had been building digital flight simulators since the 60s. But the use of *virtual* had a trippy allure that wasn't present with its rival *artificial*, which figured in phrases like *artificial intelligence. Artificial* just referred to the computer's ability to simulate offline reality, with the implication that life was elsewhere. *Virtual*, on the other hand, suggested that the machines could not only imitate life but create an alternate reality of their own. It was an appealing notion to a public that had been primed by video games, by the cyberspace novels of William Gibson, and by the 1982 movie *Tron*, the first of that world-in-the-computer genre that would reach its full flower in movies like *The Matrix* and in all those Intel Inside commercials.

That was all it took to open the floodgates. Look at the way people are using *virtual* now and you have the sense of a vast phantom world assembling itself on the other side of the screen. There are virtual banks full of virtual money, virtual universities full of virtual classrooms, virtual malls full of virtual stores with virtual shelves and virtual shopping carts, virtual libraries full of virtual books published by virtual publishers. The virtual police are tracking down virtual rapists and virtual trespassers. You see references to virtual sculpture, which usually involves computer renderings of three-dimensional objects, and to virtual poetry, which I have some trouble distinguishing from the old-fashioned sort. And people even talk about "virtual facsimiles." When I first saw that one, it had the sound of a major metaphysical breakthrough. It was a little disappointing to realize it refers to a fax you send via your PC.

The striking thing about *virtual* is the way it slips between the real and the fictitious without tipping its hand. When the techno-enthusiasts use an expression like "virtual voter" they're referring to real voters who use the Internet. For them, it's just one of the new categories created by technology that are going to transform social life — virtual communities, virtual town halls, or the "virtual commons," a kind of general assembly area for the republic of pixels. For critics, though, the phrase "virtual voter" is more likely to be a phantom voter created by computer fraud. For them, the adjective usually signals technology's ability to create deceptive simulations and illusions, as in the title of a recent book called *Resisting the Virtual Life*.

In fact neither party uses the adjective according to its traditional meaning. For the enthusiasts it no longer suggests any reservation about truth or actuality, the way *virtual* does in a phrase like "a virtual cure for the common cold." And for the critics it doesn't have the implication that the virtual is an effective substitute for the real. But there's a common thread in the way everybody uses *virtual*, too. Whether the things you're talking about are real or fictitious, the adjective always suggests a kind of digital exceptionality — the idea that the effects of the technology are so singular and so powerful that we need a new word to describe them.

Not long ago, a young man in Florida was arrested for sending a threatening message via an Internet chat group to one of the survivors of the Columbine massacre. The young man's lawyer announced that his client was going to plead that he was the victim of an addiction to the Internet, and claim that his message was a "virtual threat made in a virtual state of mind." That seemed something of a stretch, even for a word as elastic as *virtual*. But it's a natural extension of the frenzy for discerning new virtualities whenever a new button pops up on a screen. Everything that happens online seems to be unprecedented, answering to its own virtual logic. You think of the way people were blaming the Littleton killings themselves on video games that promoted "virtual violence," or on Internet sites that had created a "virtual Munich Beer Hall" for disaffected teenagers. So why not make special allowances for the fantasies that people act out in virtual states of mind? It's a new world in there.

# Hackers {2000}

There's a Gresham's law of language, too — the bad senses drive out the good ones. *Senile* used to mean just "old," and *silly* started out its life meaning "harmless." A junket was originally just a party.

Or take the word *hack*, as in "hack writer" or "a hack job." That's originally a shortening of *hackney*, which referred to a horse that was easy to ride — it came from the Hackney area of London, where horses were raised in the Middle Ages. From there it came to refer to a horse kept for hire (that's where we get the use of *hack* to mean cab driver), then to anyone who hires himself out to do low or servile jobs. (In Shakespeare's time, in fact, the words *hack* and *hackney* were synonyms for "prostitute.") From there it became a description for any incompetent work, as in "a hack job." And finally *hackneyed* came to mean a tired phrase that's in promiscuous use.

These uses of *hack* had only an indirect influence on the way computer programmers started using *hack* and *hacker* back in the 1960s. Probably the new use owed as much to the use of *hack* to mean "chop," which was what had given rise to phrases like "tennis hacker," and it may owe something to "hacking around," too. (Actually it's often hard to say just which sense of a word a new slang term is based on — new senses tend to resonate up and down the dictionary entry.) But like the older senses of *hack*, these words started out as positive terms, part of the cult language that grew up among programmers in the early days of computer science at places like MIT and Carnegie-Mellon. When you hear a programmer say, "She can really hack," it's in the appreciative tone that a jazz musician uses when he says, "He can really blow."

In recent years, though, *hacker* has gone down the same steep road that *hack* and *hackney* took a couple of hundred years ago. The process started early on. Already in the 60s, engineering students were using *hack* to refer to an ingenious prank, which might involve a computer-system break-in. Sometimes these were just irrepressible student hijinks, sometimes they were more malicious acts by programmer wannabes. And when those break-ins began to make headlines in the 80s, the press naturally took the term *hackers* to describe the perpetrators, to the point where that's the only sense of the word that most people are aware of now.

A lot of programmers get indignant about this use of the word. They insist that *hacker* should be used only as a term of praise, and they suggest that *crackers* should be used to describe the people who do malicious break-ins, which among other things don't usually involve exceptional programming skill. I appreciate their point, but there's no possibility that the process will be reversed, no more than *hackney* is going to go back to meaning a horse that's easy to ride. For one thing, the public likes to believe that the intruder-hackers are an exceptionally clever lot. After all, the alternative would be a lot more frightening — if any high school dropout with a modem and a grudge can bring down the NASDAQ server, then we're really in trouble. And in fact there has been a kind of complicity between the press and the perpetrators themselves to portray the hacker with a certain sinister allure, for example in John Markoff's bestseller *Takedown,* a nonfiction thriller about the escapades and eventual capture of the arch-hacker Kevin Mitnick, or the 1995 film *Hackers*, with Angelina Jolie playing the ringleader of a bunch of angry misfits with exotic aliases who break into corporate servers and uncover fiendish criminal schemes.

Of course most programmers don't bear much resemblance to the hacker stereotype of the precocious sociopath. (They don't bear a lot of resemblance to Angelina Jolie, either.) But you can see why there's a temptation to seize on the image of the hacker as an emblem of the entire breed. When you're sitting there unable to log in to your stockbroker while your portfolio tanks, you're not usually in the mood to care whether the problem is due to the wanton and deliberate mischief of some hacker or the purely inadvertent mischief that ordinary programmers work in the course of writing hundreds of thousands of lines of code. For most people, it's a little vexing to realize that the smooth operation of our economy is at the mercy of a tribe of impudent twenty-somethings in ponytails and Converse sneakers who regard the rest of us with undisguised condescension. Every time I have to call in to the help desk of some software company or online service, I have the sense of being cast in a recurring episode from the old *Sky King* TV series — the one where the pilot of a small plane has passed out and someone in the control tower is trying to talk his eight-year-old passenger in for a landing. "Now Billy, I want you to pull back *slowly* on that stick in front of you. That's *good*, Billy!"

I've noticed that a lot of programmers have taken to using *hacker* with the negative sense that everyone else assigns to the word. Partly I suppose it's because they realize that they've been fighting a losing battle on this one. But it also reflects a kind of demystification of their trade as programming becomes a more commodified skill and all that talk about the "hacker code" comes to sound a little precious. In the end, that's always what happens to the cults that emerge among the early practitioners of new technologies, from the steamboat to the telegraph to the airplane. Programmers can at least have the consolation of knowing that the same process works to temper the villainous specters that also grow up around those technologies — the Frankensteins, the Dr. Strangeloves, or the demoniacal hackers of the recent headlines. It isn't that hacking is about to disappear anytime soon, but as time passes it will be just another of the hackneyed criminalities of modern life.

# business talk

# You're Out of Here    {1996}

**M**r. Dithers could allow himself the luxury of directness: "Bumstead, you're fired!" But nowadays the axe is so muffled you can barely hear it fall. Xerox announced "involuntary force reductions," while at Digital Equipment there were "involuntary methodologies." Tandem Computers did "focussed reductions," and the people at Sun Oil said they were "managing down" their "staff resources." ("Bumstead, you're managed down!")

Ideally, though, corporations like to describe the process as a kind of fitness regime for the body corporate, rather than focus on its effects on the individual cells. Companies are restructured, re-engineered, redeployed, rightshaped, and of course downsized. Ramada Inns has been "streamlining," National Semiconductor tried "reshaping." *Lean* is a favorite word here — "a new, leaner Sears Roebuck." It's a good choice — it makes you think of Scottie Pippen driving the line, not some emaciated guy cadging change at the corner.

Of course there have always been lots of synonyms for "dismiss," but before this century they were the graveyard humor of the people who found themselves at the business end of the boot. Maybe that's why these expressions are mostly used in the passive. You "get canned," "get axed," "get the boot," "get the sack" (the origins of that one are lost back in the seventeenth century). Or of course you "get fired," which originated in the late nineteenth century as a pun on *discharged* — both being things you do with a gun.

But people didn't really start to euphemize the process until the 1930s or so, when the expression "let go" made its first appearance. This was the first of these phrases to take the employer's point of view. That's why it's always used with *have to*, as in

"We're going to have to let you go, Carruthers." It puts you in mind of a captive bird scraping at the door of his cage. Still, it's excessively apologetic for the modern corporation, which prefers to leave the employees unmentioned.

It's a good rule that when you hear a euphemism you can be pretty sure there's a sense of shame lurking somewhere just out of sight. And maybe that's really the new element here. Losing your job has always been a cause for anger and fear, but it's only in recent times that people have come to think of it as somehow shameful — as if firing people is an assault not just on their livelihood but on their identity as well. As the management consultant Jack Lawrence put it, "People are what they do nowadays, because they're not sure what else to be" — particularly if they're the loyal middle managers who have been the most conspicuous victims of the latest rounds of restructuring.

This at least is the message sent out by all these frantic corporate efforts to find new terms for the same old stories — as if to say, "We aren't really doing this." And not surprisingly, this kind of talk has exacerbated the public indignation over the restructurings themselves. In the public eye, in fact, corporations have pretty much replaced the government as the chief perpetrators of doublespeak and jargon over the past five or ten years, which is saying something.

It's tempting to personalize the outrage; you want to think that it reflects a rising tide of insincerity and deviousness. But doublespeak isn't usually an individual transgression: it's what happens when the system itself begins to talk. If there is an invisible hand that manages the marketplace, there sometimes seems to be an invisible mouth that speaks for it. You can decide for yourself whether the current restructurings are implicit in the logic of a new global economy that mandates massive reductions in the workforce at the same time that it entails that CEO compensation packages should rise at several times the rate of inflation. But I'm certain that the publicists who coin all these euphemisms have no choice in the matter at all. It's unfortunate, it's regrettable, it could have been me. But it is really something that we would prefer not to dwell on, particularly with the Wall Street analysts attending to every nuance of the press releases.

Corporate language is exactly like the corporation itself — both are fictions created in order to limit individual responsibility. That's what makes modern corporations different from Mr. Dithers' little office: it's nothing personal.

# Whaddya Know? {1998}

In a sense, the knowledge management craze originated with T. S. Eliot's famous lines from "The Rock":

> Where is the Life we have lost in living?
> Where is the wisdom we have lost in knowledge?
> Where is the knowledge we have lost in information?

But that sententious pessimism is out of line with modern technocratic thinking. It was left to Al Gore to give the story the upbeat turn it needed, in a speech he first gave around 1990. Gore took Eliot's *wisdom*, *knowledge*, and *information*, threw in a couple of other terms like *data* and *understanding*, and arranged them in a golden chain of added value: "Our challenge is to process data into information, refine information into knowledge, extract from knowledge understanding and then let understanding ferment into wisdom."

This was a vision that technologists and managers could love, with humanity progressing up the ladder rather than down it. Actually the rungs of the ladder have been assembling for the last couple of decades. That data-into-information business first caught on in the 70s, as a way of talking about the added value of systems like graphical user interfaces and automatic spreadsheets, which promised to make data more comprehensible. In fact the definition of information as processed data had no real scientific basis. The "information" that computers traffic in is just the stuff of bits and bandwidth, and has nothing to do with the sort of meaningful content that we have in mind when we talk about the "information economy" and the like. From a technical point of view, there is no more information in a *New York Times* article than in "Jabberwocky," and for that matter there is more information in a table of random numbers than in either of those. But it was a compelling rhetorical turn, which helped to sell a lot of software. And in fact the definition of information as processed knowledge has even managed to work its way into some dictionaries, which I suppose makes it true.

The only problem was that all the information technology that organizations were deploying didn't seem to be producing any dramatic productivity gains. One popular theory about this failure was that information by itself wasn't enough to turn the trick — it just piled up in individual cubicles where nobody knew how to find it or how to make it useful. That was what led the management gurus to grab on to the next rung of the ladder, and establish the new cult of knowledge. It's like the difference between "medical information" and "medical knowledge" — with the first you think of a collection of facts and figures; with the second you think of a community that can put the information to use.

Out of that eminently reasonable hypothesis grew the knowledge craze. When it comes to being slaves to fashion, American managers make adolescent girls look like rugged individualists. Before long every boardroom and business journal was buzzing with phrases like "knowledge assets," "knowledge ecology," "knowledge creation," and "knowledge sharing." The vendors of everything from email software to web search tools are billing their products as "knowledge management systems." More than a hundred companies in the Fortune 500 have established a post of Chief Knowledge Officer, and at Berkeley they've even established a Distinguished Professorship in Knowledge (as it happens, it's in the Business School, but I guess the chair could have gone to any department).

It's true that these people are working on real problems, and a lot of these schemes and systems will lead to real productivity gains. But it isn't clear how much the word *knowledge* will contribute to this — it has become a mantra that people chant hopefully over their shrinkwrap and reorganization charts. And it's in the nature of these fads to be evanescent — it's a fair bet that "knowledge management" will not outlive the Spice Girls. Before long the term *knowledge* will wind up on the dust heap of history alongside of the linguistic detritus of other management vogues — words like *quality*, *empowerment*, and *corporate culture*. Management gurus are a restless lot who treat the English vocabulary as an inexhaustible resource; they go through it like Brazilian farmers burning their way through the rain forest. And there's no shortage of new words to appropriate as they work their way up the value-added ladder. The other day I read an interview with a sociologist who was saying, "Contemporary wisdom research is in its infancy," and I could picture the gleam in her eye.

It struck me that this might be a good place to get in on the ground floor. I didn't see myself carving out a second career in wisdomology, but maybe it wasn't too late to register some of the web domain names that people are sure to start looking for in a couple of years. But as with most of my million-dollar schemes, I was way behind the curve. It turned out that the domain name *wisdom.com* has already been grabbed by a Louisiana outfit that sells web products, and *understanding.com* is registered to a company that puts together software tutorials. In desperation I even tried *enlightenment.com*, but it was taken by someone else. I'd love to tell you what they do, but when I went searching for enlightenment, the server wasn't responding.

# Slides Rule    {1999}

**S**cott McNealy, the CEO at Sun Micro, never misses an opportunity to try to stick it to Microsoft. A couple of years ago he went so far as to try to ban the use of Power-Point at Sun, claiming that employees were wasting colossal amounts of time preparing slides. It was a dramatic gesture, but this is one tide that isn't about to roll back on command. PowerPoint and other kinds of presentation software are ubiquitous wherever business people meet to communicate ... well, I was about to say "face to face," but that isn't quite accurate when everybody's staring at the screen. The technology has even created a new unit of measure for meting out access to senior management. It used to be that you got ten minutes of the CEO's time; now you get three slides to make your pitch.

Inevitably, the ability to prepare a slide presentation has become an indispensable corporate survival skill. Rank novices can start with the templates that come with the software, such as "Reporting Progress" (Kandinsky-like blue and red rectangles) or "Communicating Bad News" (a suggestive shade of brown). And corporations provide master slides with approved fonts, colors, and logos, along with helpful design guidelines. The Bank of America counsels employees to keep slides to no more than two fonts or seven lines of text so as to avoid the ransom-note look that's a sure sign of the slide-show neophyte. But most managers have come to realize that slides are too important to pick off the rack or to leave entirely to the discretion of the creative services people. It's remarkable how quickly they've come up to speed. Corporate types whose interest in media aesthetics used to be limited to watching Siskel and Ebert have become adept at discussing the use of once-arcane filmic effects like builds, dissolves, and wipes.

Some people, of course, are too old or too busy to learn the new tricks. For them there's always the postmodern ploy of appropriation, a strategy favored by a lot of senior managers. It gives employees even more of an incentive to come up with dazzling slides, in the hope that a couple of them might work their way into the boss's presentations. In the modern corporation, an effective slide can be a commodity as much in demand as a Nolan Ryan rookie card.

For some, the presentation software explosion is just one more sign of the general decline in public speaking — as Cliff Nass, a Stanford professor of communications, put it, "Try to imagine the 'I have a dream' speech in PowerPoint." But it isn't as if that tradition was exactly flourishing before PowerPoint came along. It's a long way down from King's address to Ross Perot's TV charts (a medium he doubtless mastered in his early days at IBM, the Fertile Crescent of the presentation culture). And you have to give the benefit of the doubt to any technology that promises to make the average corporate presentation a less numbing experience than it used to be.

Anyway, slides aren't intended to be merely accompaniments to talks anymore — they're increasingly taking on a life of their own. These days no one asks for a memo or report anymore; now it's just "Send me your slides." Conferences post the slides of their speakers' talks, and professors post the slides of their lectures. Even the clergy have begun to post slides of their sermons on the web for the benefit of anyone who was unable to attend the service.

True, it isn't always easy to make sense of slides in isolation — it can be like trying to reconstruct the social life of ancient Pompeii from the graffiti its inhabitants left behind. But that hasn't stopped the format from spreading to other genres.

The recent releases of PowerPoint let you use the software to produce homepages and other web documents. And the presentation format has even made inroads in the book, the last bastion of connected prose. The other day I went to the business section of a local bookstore and started opening books at random. I had to do this twelve times before I came to two facing pages of text that were uninterrupted by a subhead, illustration, figure, sidebar, pull quote, or some other graphic distraction.

Like the book and other communications technologies of the past, this one is having its effects on the structure of thought itself. The more PowerPoint presentations you prepare, the more the world seems to package itself into slide-sized chunks, broken down into bullet items or grouped in geometric patterns that have come to have an almost talismanic force. A friend of mine who works for a large Silicon Valley company maintains that no proposal can win management buy-in until it has been reduced to three items placed along the sides of a triangle.

You could think of all this as the new illumination. In a lot of ways we've become the most visual culture since the High Middle Ages. And there are times when I look at PowerPoint presentations and recall the stained-glass windows of Gothic cathedrals, a series of images that could evoke a complex narrative for the illiterate faithful.

Still, we probably don't want to toss out all the achievements of the age of print. There are some useful communicative tools that are left behind in the move from connected text to bullet items (verbs, for example). And as lively as a good slide show can be, there are some ideas that are better communicated in a more leisurely, discursive way, with the aid of older technologies like an armchair and a good reading light.

# Come Together, Right Now  {1999}

*Convergence* has an impeccable pedigree: it was coined as a Latin term in the early seventeenth century by no less estimable an authority than Johannes Kepler in his work on optics, and found its way into English about a hundred years later. Over the next few centuries it did quiet scholarly work describing the behavior of rays of light, astronomical bodies, and those ingenious mathematical series that enabled Achilles finally to catch up with the tortoise that the Greek philosopher Zeno had despaired of his ever being able to reach, since he would have had to first cover half the distance, then half of the remainder, and so on.

Of course *convergence* has been making appearances in ordinary language for a long time — Flannery O'Connor used it in the title of her famous short story "Everything That Rises Must Converge," about a shabby-genteel Southern white family bemused by the blurrings of racial and social boundaries in the New South. But the word wasn't brought out for a star turn until 1987, the date of the Great Harmonic Convergence, when thousands of rainbow humans flocked to Mount Shasta, Stonehenge, Central Park, and other magnetic vortices to create a sense of attunement to the galactic intelligences. At the time it was not clear just what was supposed to be converging — the planets (which would have been better described as aligning) or the participants (who would have been better described as shuffling in). In any event, the word was soon attached to other convocations of alternative life- and body-styles — there are annual "convergences" of Net Goths and overweight men — as well as to a magazine devoted to "resources for exploring life as a spiritual journey."

There was something vaguely New Agey, too, in the way

the word became popular around this time to describe the coming together of disciplines, media, cultures, and technologies, usually with the implication that they are all swept along by some leveling global wind that's picking up as we approach Y2K. When a word starts to buzz, it vibrates everywhere — as soon as *convergence* was in the air, the world seemed to be full of things that called out to be described by it. There were new interdisciplinary scientific fields like neurolinguistics and sociobiology; new musical styles like Afropop, heavy-metal techno, and just plain "world"; new entertainment genres like infomercials and advertorials.

More than anything else, though, *convergence* has seemed an ideal word to describe the effects of information technology, which throws together disciplines, products, and businesses that used to have nothing in common. Informatization has made computer jockeys out of musicians and artists. (Advice from the painter Gregory Amenoff to the graduating class of the Ringling School of Art in Sarasota last year: "I have just one word for you as you set out on your artistic careers ... Photoshop.") It has fed a mania for mergers and alliances among purveyors of traditional content, telecommunications and cable and Internet services, all angling toward the day when everything from movies to medical records will be plying the same digital ocean. And it has set heads in consumer industries dancing with visions of the universal appliance — I think of it as a digital Veg-E-Matic — that will make it possible to misplace a single device behind the cushions of your couch and thereby cut off your access not just to the TV and the stereo but also to your email, your stockbroker, your family photo album, and your garage door.

But while all of these could be described as convergences of one sort or another, it isn't as if they have any common significance. Nor are any of them unprecedented. Scientific and cultural traditions have always been coming together (that's what gave us astrophysics, organic chemistry, and jazz), and new basic technologies have always created links among previously unrelated tools — who before the late nineteenth century would have thought that trains had anything in common with toasters? What's different now is not so much the nature of the phenomena, or even, despite all the talk of the "ever-accelerating pace of change," their number or rapidity. It's that unlike previous generations we feel the need to lump them together under a single name.

In part, all this talk of convergences is simply a response to the anxiety that shifting category boundaries always evoke, whether in the Silicon Valley of the 90s or the New South of the 60s. But if that were all there is to it, other words would probably do as well. Depending on the details of the case in question, we could talk about unifications, fusions, mergers, integrations, hybridizations, or blendings, with no implication that any of them signaled an epochal trend.

What *convergence* adds is a note of determinism, a sense that all these categories are moving together on paths as definite as the planetary orbits. It's a perfect fit for the chiliastic rhetoric of modern-day visionaries, whether they're writing in *The Watchtower* or *Wired* — the sense that things are rapidly headed toward some millenarian rapture that will bring salvation to those who extrapolate the trends correctly and destruction to the laggards who ignore the footsteps behind them, as convergence does to them what it did to Zeno's tortoise. At the least, it makes for an appealing story for companies to tell the analysts by way of justifying acquisitions and forays into new product lines — on Wall Street, the operating assumption seems to be that everything that converges must rise.

But like stock bubbles, linguistic vogues have a way of bursting when they are stretched too thin. It's likely that *convergence* will have as short a half-life as most others, not just because its novelty will wear off in time, but because it tends to obscure the nature of most of the changes that people apply it to — not just their ultimate unpredictabililty, but the way they work to create new distinctions and categories even as they are eradicating old ones.

Think about the great category shifts of the past. In retrospect, we wouldn't say that the work of Einstein and Bohr led to the convergence of physics and chemistry or that the development of the internal combustion engine led to a convergence of horseless carriages and chain saws. Nor, despite Flannery O'Connor's ironic title, did the social movements of the 60s lead to the convergence of the races or the sexes; on the contrary, we find ourselves with an astonishing range of new social identities and with more distinct genders than anyone could have imagined in the age of *Father Knows Best*.

Things converge, but they also diverge and reverge (a pity that Kepler never got around to inventing that verb, which would have come in handy now). And for all that it's easier to perceive the disappearance of old boundaries than the emergence of new ones, it isn't as if people aren't aware of this. After all, the same age that made *convergence* a buzzword has also brought late-career stardom to that old word *niche*.

# It's the Thought That Matters   {2000}

**A** while ago I got an invitation to participate in a workshop on the future of knowledge, as part of a group of distinguished thought leaders. Needless to say, I accepted. "Thought leader" — nobody ever called me that before. I had half a mind to put it down under "occupation" the next time I have to fill out a credit application.

It turns out, unfortunately, that my new status isn't quite as exclusive or as novel as I'd hoped. The phrase "thought leader" started its life around twenty years ago as a bit of marketing jargon to describe the sort of person who reads magazines like the *New Republic* or the *Atlantic*. At its inception it meant pretty much the same thing as "opinion maker," which was the marketing jargon of the previous generation. But over the past few years the phrase has been spreading itself around much more widely, and now it's used for anybody who's thought to have influence over the way people think. Management consultants routinely describe themselves as "recognized international thought leaders," generally with some phrase like "learning communities" or "change agents" within a comma's throw. An insurance company describes itself as a thought leader in long-term care, and I found a webpage some consultant had put up that described Socrates as the first thought leader of knowledge management.

It turns out I was scooped on using "thought leader" as an occupational title, too. I ran into a job listing for a software company that was looking for a thought leader for its retail sales division and offering a salary in the 100–120K range. The ad didn't say what the job qualifications were, but it's a safe bet that a facility with PowerPoint came into the picture somewhere.

I'm not about to begrudge anybody a job title that commands a six-figure salary. Still, there's something a little clumsy about the phrase. It feels like it should be in German — *Gedankenführer*. It's an awkwardness that seems to be endemic when we try to come up with words to talk about people who traffic in ideas. When "thought leader" and "opinion maker" were first introduced, after all, they were just expedients for avoiding the word *intelligentsia*, probably because nobody was sure how to pronounce it.

An article in *Newsweek* last fall suggested that we think of thought leaders as something like "lay intellectuals," but *intellectual* is a word with problems of its own. Americans are comfortable using it as an adjective when they're talking about property or a stimulating conversation. But when *intellectual* is used as a noun it conjures up the image of woolly academics swollen with self-importance — when I did a search in a newspaper database, I was struck by how often the word *intellectual* was modified by phrases like "self-styled" and "so-called." That was the attitude that George W. Bush was appealing to a while ago when he was answering questions about his poor college grades and his somewhat rudimentary grasp of geography and international politics. "I was never a great intellectual," he said, sounding pretty confident that the American electorate wouldn't hold that failing against him. In fact I wouldn't be surprised if Gore is asked to make the same pledge before the campaign is out. The last successful presidential candidate who would have owned up to being an intellectual was Woodrow Wilson, but that was back in an age when college teaching and football were still gentlemen's games.

Some commentators have been trying to get around this lingering prejudice by making the case for what they call "public intellectuals." The phrase is usually associated with a nostalgia for the age of those mid-twentieth-century thinkers who could talk to a wider audience without having clouds of chalk dust issue from their mouths — people like John Dewey, Edmund Wilson, or Lewis Mumford. I suspect that Wilson himself would have been dismayed by the phrase "public intellectual," but I can understand the desire to make American intellectuals seem sexier, more like the way intellectuals are regarded in France, where talk-show producers have Rolodexes full of historians and philosophers with Bee Gees hairdos who can appear on half an hour's notice and deliver themselves of exquisitely worded opinions on anything from mad cow disease to gangsta rap. If Noam Chomsky were French, he would be known to the public just as NC and wouldn't have to wait for a table in a fancy restaurant. (The French even have a slang word for intellectuals — *les intellos*. That couldn't happen here; it would be like having a slang word for chemical engineers.)

In the end, though, I suspect that the phrase "public intellectual" is fighting a hopeless rear-guard battle. The future belongs to the thought leaders. At least I've noticed that while sociologists and political scientists still like to describe themselves as intellectuals, the business school gurus who command the five-figure speaking fees have gone over to calling themselves thought leaders. That's probably all it takes to put the phrase over the top in the marketplace of ideas.

# A Name Too Far   {2000}

**W**hen General Electric's legendary CEO Jack Welsh re-
tires in a few months, the business press will be full of
tributes to the man who took a sleepy electrical products
company and turned it into the corporation with the world's
largest market value. One thing Welsh probably won't get
credit for, though, is having the sense not to change the corporation's name. The temptation would be understandable;
after all, light bulbs and appliances are only a small part of
the GE conglomerate, which includes everything from financial services to truck leasing to NBC. And it isn't as if
Welsh has shown exquisite linguistic instincts up and down
the line. This is a corporation that gave its famous quality-
control program the name Six Sigma, which sounds like a
term L. Ron Hubbard would come up with.

Still, for every old-economy company that hangs on to its
name, like GE or Caterpillar or Minnesota Mining and Manu-
facturing, there seem to be five that are pitching it over the side.
Occasionally the change makes sense — when there's a merger,
or when the old name acquires some unfortunate associations.
A year after the ValueJet air crash that killed a hundred people, the company bought a small carrier called AirTrans and
painted that name on all its planes. And after the Johns Manville people paid out a couple of billion dollars to settle asbestos
claims in the 80s, they decided to lie low for a while under the
name of the Schuller Corporation, before going back to Johns
Manville about three years ago, when the dust had cleared. But
most of the new corporate names are just an attempt to liven up
a tired brand with a little linguistic nip and tuck — and in fact
you see a lot of perfectly healthy companies doing this in the

same spirit with which they roll out a new advertising campaign every couple of years.

The one thing you can be sure of is that whatever the reason for picking a new corporate name, it will be more fanciful and less descriptive than the old one. This might be simply a consequence of the outsourcing process. When you pay several hundred thousand dollars to a corporate identity consultant with a gaggle of linguists and marketing specialists on its staff, you don't expect them to come back with the suggestion that you call yourself U.S. Tanks and Boilers. You want syllables that buzz with the promise of marketing magic. You go from International Harvester to Navistar, Advanced Medical to Alaris, Inter Regional Financial Group to Interra.

But all these names tend to blur, since they give you no sense at all of what the companies actually do. Take Agilent, the name that Hewlett-Packard created when it spun off its original core businesses of making measurement devices and instrumentation. Evidently the idea was to suggest agility, but that's not a feature you generally look for in an oscilloscope — it's more like what you want in a roofer. Mainly the object seems to have been to come up with one of those trendy adjectival names that end in *−ent* and *−ant* — companies like Teligent, Sapient, Viant, Naviant, Novient, Noviant. There are fashions in these things the way there are in the names of retail stores; one year the malls are full of Trouser Shacks and Umbrella Shacks, the next year they've all turned into huts, the year after that they're marts.

For all their talk about brand differentiation, corporate identity consultants are basically herd animals. It seems as if eighty percent of high-tech start-ups get their names from the same formula — they take a prefix like *digi−*, *inter−*, or *info−*, tack on a suffix like *−vision*, *−cast*, or *−web*, and throw in an unconventional spelling or capitalization to show they've moved beyond the orthographic orthodoxies of the old economy.

Not surprisingly, the nondescript conformism of new corporate names has sparked a reaction. The latest fashion among technology start-ups is for names that have a funky, homespun feel. Redhat, Redback, Blue Pumpkin, Tumbleweed, Razorfish — it's getting hard to tell the software companies from the microbreweries. The names conjure up a bunch of Gen-Xers sitting around in a loft in T-shirts and sneakers, kids who are so far ahead of the curve that they can call themselves whatever they damn well please. But like any bandwagon, this one is easy enough for old-economy firms to jump onto. BlueLight.com, for example, turns out to be the name the Kmart people picked for their new e-commerce site. True, it's an allusion to the chain's "Blue Light Specials," but still, "Attention, BlueLight shoppers" doesn't ring right at the moment.

It's getting to the point where corporations change their names as readily as they introduce new product brands. And inevitably the process tends to feed on itself. It's a curious phenomenon of the modern marketplace that the more corporations spend on branding their products or themselves, the more brand loyalty diminishes. Stockholders, employees, consumers — they're all more fickle than they used to be. Only a sap holds on to a position for the long haul. And if the new corporate names don't work out, they're a lot easier to replace than something that's been monogrammed on your table linen for fifty or a hundred years.

I started to have some hope a year or two ago when WMX Technologies went back to its old name of Waste Management Incorporated. Now that's a fine, descriptive old-economy name — they might as well use the motto "Garbage Is Us." The only trouble is that the stock is still in the dumps.

# Having Issues  {2000}

I was watching a TV business program as the CEO of a large company was explaining why they had missed their numbers for the previous quarter. They had had an issue with their foreign markets, he said, and another issue with a sales force reorganization. But he concluded on an upbeat note. I quote: "The issue is to execute and we're going through these executional issues."

If I had to pick a single begetter of all of this "issue" talk, I'd point to Fritz Perls, the progenitor of the various shoots and stalks of the Human Potential Movement that flourished in the 70s — gestalt, transactional, existential, Esalen, and the rest. That's when we began to internalize all our external conflicts and redefine reality as a purely in-house product — "Don't look at them, look at yourself." And the effects on the language are still being played out.

Take the way we ask permission. It used to be that we said, "I'm going to take off now; is that OK with you?" Now we say, "Are you OK with that?" The end result is the same, but the perspective is inverted — the language has rotated its eyeballs one hundred eighty degrees inward. It's as if to say, "Before I leave, please tongue your psyche and see if you encounter any raw spots that might prevent you from, as it were, being there for me when I get back."

It was the same change in point of view that led people to start using *problem* as a euphemism for "disagreement" or "dislike": "I've got a problem with the way she yells at everybody." That was a major step in the annals of confrontation avoidance. Instead of expressing your opinion you could describe your inner states in a neutral, dispassionate way, like a political boss reporting the sentiment of the party faithful — "It's nothing to me one way or the other, but I'm running into some resistance in the third ward."

The only problem with *problem* is that it's redolent of a certain counterproductive negativity. When you start using the *p*-word it's only a small step to using the *b*-word, *blame*. Hence the brilliant stroke of substituting *issue*, which turns what once were obstacles into neutral talking points. When you tell somebody that there's a problem that has to be fixed, you are, as they say, personalizing your criticism. The team-oriented way to put this is to say that there's an issue that has to be revisited. I expect it's only a matter of time before I hear a baseball announcer saying, "He's a good fielder but he has an issue hitting the curve ball."

Remember when we used to dismiss this sort of talk as psychobabble? That was back in the 70s, when all these therapies and fads were having their heyday, most exuberantly out here in northern California. It's the period that Cyra McFadden satirized in her 1977 bestseller *The Serial*, which recounted a year in the life of a terminally hip couple in Marin County, just over the Golden Gate Bridge. The book engendered endless mirth in the rest of the country for its dead-on renderings of the lifestyle and language of the moment, and probably did more than anything else to establish the California joke as a fixture in late-night talk-show monologues.

It's funny, though — when you reread McFadden's novel now, the characters' enthusiasms don't strike you as nearly so absurd as they did at the time. Twenty-five years later, it's hard to recall what was so risible about being into jogging, ten-speed bicycles, ecology, cappuccino, or "Women's Lib," as people at the time used to call it. For that matter, it's not clear why we thought it was so ridiculous that McFadden's characters should be into saying "be into." Was it really only northern Californians back then who said, "You've got to get your act together" or "I was completely blown away by that"? And how about the word *process*, which the modern corporation would be hard put to live without — it brings you up short to realize that people used to consider it New Age jargon.

A quarter of a century after *The Serial* appeared, the movements that Perls inspired and McFadden satirized are mostly passé. But most of the language they left us has moved into mainstream, and nowhere more prominently than in the American corporation, where it was imported by HR people and management theorists. Once you bleached the talk of its more pointed ideological content, it turned out to be a perfect medium for blurring the hard edges of hierarchy — for bringing people on board and getting them to align with your end-state vision. We've reached the point where the CEO of a Fortune 500 company can talk about having execution issues and nobody even thinks to make a Marin County joke. We all crossed that bridge some time ago.

# valediction

# Pack It In!  {1999}

**B**efore we start on the carousin'
We've planned to greet the year two thousan',
Let's empty our linguistic closets
Of their detritus and deposits
And sweep our storerooms, in the bargain,
Of solecisms, slang, and jargon.
Then, as the afternoon gets late,
Let's dump it from the Golden Gate,
And with one stroke, bold and defiant,
Make English Y2K-compliant.

Let's clear out our congested cargo
Of business cant and corporate argot.
We'll ditch *proactive* for a starter,
And "We don't work harder, just work smarter"
(A phrase that was cooked up, my hunch is,
To justify two-hour lunches).
*Synergistic* or *synergetic*? —
Either one gives me a headache,
And the notion of convergence
Is in need of some submergence.
Let's ditch *road warrior* (save when jocular);
Ditto *vision* (save when ocular).
Consign *restructure* to the void,
And *downsize* should be redeployed
(At least, the next time we get canned,
We'll know exactly where we stand).

Let's lose *win-win*, that favorite phrase
Of hearty Harvard MBAs,

And cast on the outgoing tide
The box they like to think outside,
In hopes that in the coming age
We'll all be on a different page.

It wasn't very long ago
The Internet was *comme il faut*,
And only the most avant-garde
Had @-signs on their business card.
But now that even Aunt Estelle
Has got herself a URL,
And Vinnie at the barbershop
Made millions on his first-day pop,
We've reached the point where talking geekish
Is starting to sound so last weekish.
*Emoticon* and *digerati*
Aren't worth a wooden zloty.
To *portal* we can give the gate,
*Mindshare* will do for tuna bait,
And since you asked, IMHO,
Those email acronyms are *de trop.*
And ere the sun sets, let us jettison
*Newbie*, *netiquette*, and *netizen*,
Nor should we miss this opportunity
To deep-six *virtual community*,
e-this, i-that, and without qualm,
Let's unplug everything.com.

On literary critics' patois
I think we must declare a fatwah:
It's hard to part with *hegemonic*,
But in the end you'll find it tonic;
Think how much more ribald reading's rendered

When it is sexed instead of gendered,
And curling up at bedtime, who wants
To be holding something nuanced?
Of that *du jour* contraction *pomo*,
I'd just as soon that we heard no mo',
Nor any others of the host
Of vocables prefixed with *post*–.
We seem to be, for all our fears,
Still modern after all these years.

I'm sure that ages hence will honor us
If we stop cooking up new genres,
Let's spare the coming centuries
Prequels and rockumentaries,
And pause not even for a comma
Before discarding *docudrama*.
And ere the clock chimes, let us vow
That critics twenty years from now
Will earn themselves an instant wedgie
Whenever they use *taut* or *edgy*.

Before we can put on our nightcaps,
We've other words to feed the whitecaps:
Let's leave off calling rumors *buzz*,
And blow off anyone who does.
*Wake-up call* has gotten thin —
Next year we'll all be sleeping in.
And anything you feel like sharing
Kindly offer to the herring.

And as we're chucking out the dross,
Make sure we don't neglect to toss
Those interjections, coy and clever —

Like "Let's not go there" and "Whatever!"
(And while we're at it, do I gotta
Even mention "Yadda yadda"?)
*Arrivederci* to "Ex-*cuse* me";
You simply no longer amuse me.
Farewell to "Duh!" and, apropos,
Let's say buh-bye now to "Hell-*o?*"

Now as we watch the century go out,
There's only one more thing to throw out:
Let's cast onto the coastal shelf
The word *millennium* itself.
(I'm glad to bid that one adieu —
The fact is that I never knew
If it should have one *n* or two.)

And as night falls on the Presidio,
Let's all go home and watch a video,
To pass the century's final hour
(That is, assuming we've got power).

# Subject Index

Hewlett-Packard, 33, 224
Higgins, George V., 61, 63
Hindus, 83
Hirsch, E.D., 144, 167
Hitler, Adolf, 67
Hoffman, Abbie, 114
Hollerith, Dr. Herman, 131, 132
Holzer, Jenny, 196
Hope, Bob, 59
Hubbard, L. Ron, 83, 223
Hughes, Robert, 77
humor, 91
Hunt, Leigh, 70
Hussein, Saddam, 103

IBM, 132, 152, 176, 177, 214
information technology, 210–212, 217
interjections, 26–28
Internet, 99, 155, 173, 176–177, 181–183, 185, 187–189, 197, 200

Jackson, Jesse, 120
Jacquard, Joseph-Marie, 132
James, Henry, 138, 145, 147, 161, 163
James, P.D., 61
Jameson, Frederick, 30
Jarmusch, Jim, 23
jazz, 73
Jefferson, Thomas, 57
Jehovah's Witnesses, 82
jobs, losing, 207–209
Johnson, Philip, 29
Johnson, Samuel, 155, 158
Jolie, Angelina, 202
Jones, George, 47, 48, 49

Jones, Paula, 151
Jonestown Temple, 83
Joyce, James, 48, 145, 159

Kafka, Franz, 184
Kant, Immanuel, 114
Kasparov, Gary, 178, 180
Keats, John, 70, 72
Kelly, Alvin "Ship-wreck," 89
Kepler, Johannes, 216, 219
King, Larry, 9, 16, 17
King, Rodney, 103, 104
Kinsley, Michael, 184
Kipling, Rudyard, 108, 110
Kitchener, General, 107, 108
Knight, Bobby, 55
Koons, Jeff, 92
Korean War, 84
Krupp von Bohlen und Halbach, Frau Bertha, 76

Lajoie, Nap, 32
language/language criti-cism, 8, 154–156, 178–180. *See also* communications, business; grammar, rules of; writing
Lanza, Mario, 24
LaRosa, Julius, 24
Latin, 23–25
Lawrence, Jack, 208
Lawrence, T.E., 110
Leary, Timothy, 173
Lennon, John, 44
Lester, Richard, 68
Letterman, David, 92
Levinson, Barry, 69
Levittown (Long Island), 70

Lewinsky, Monica, 122
Lewis, Jerry, 89, 90
Lieberman, Senator Joseph, 125–127
Lighter, Jonathan, 73
Ligorio, Pirro, 197
Lincoln, Abraham, 112, 115, 116
Littleton killings, 195, 200
Llewellyn, William, 55
Lodge, David, 161
losing jobs, 207–209
Louis XVIII, King of France, 60
Ludd, Ned, 76
Luddites, 77, 78
Lynch, Charles, 76
lynchings, 76, 94

Macintyre, Ben, 66
Mailer, Norman, 73, 74, 75
Manet, Edouard, 50
Mao Tse-tung, 112
marketing, 44–46
Markoff, John, 202
Martin, Dean, 24
Martin, Steve, 29
Martin, Tony, 24
Marx, Karl, 106, 112
Masefield, John, 62
Masons, 82
Mastroianni, Marcello, 79
MacArthur, General Douglas, 164
McCollum, Bill, 123, 124
McFadden, Cyra, 227, 228
McNealy, Scott, 213
Melville, Herman, 161
Mencken, H.L., 45
Mfume, Kweisi, 118
Michelangelo Buonar-roti, 197

Microsoft, 33, 46, 184, 190, 213
Milgrim, Stanley, 140
Miller, Roger, 47
Milne, A.A., 25, 143
Miranda, Carmen, 21
Mitnick, Kevin, 202
modernism, 29–31
Mondragon, Joe, 73
Moon Sun Young, 83
Moore, Lorrie, 162
Mormons, 83
Morse, Samuel, 50
motion pictures, impact on language, 41–43
Motorola, 33, 46
Moyers, Bill, 9
Mulligan, Gerry, 73
Mumford, Lewis, 70, 71, 222
Murphy, Cullen, 168
Murray, Bill, 11, 12
Murray, James, 157
museums, 38
music, country, 47–49

Nabokov, Vladimir, 48
names
  for boys/girls, 3–5
  brand, 224–225
  of clothing, 106, 108
  as common nouns, 76–78
  for corporations, 223–226
  places/inhabitants of, 55–57, 109–111
Napoleon Bonaparte, 60
Nass, Cliff, 214
Nazis, 67
*New York Times* (newspaper), 23
*New York World* (newspaper), 80, 81
Newman, Edwin, 8
Nicholson, Gary, 47
nicknames, 55–57

Nietzsche, Elisabeth, 66, 67
Nietzsche, Friedrich, 66, 67, 68, 142
nouns, as verbs, 151–153, 155
Novak, Robert, 16
Nunberg, Sophie, 3–5, 143–145

Oakland (CA), 118–121
O'Connor, Flannery, 216, 219
October 1917, Revolution of, 173, 175
Olds, Bruce, 151
Olsten, William, 137
online. *See* Internet
Orwell, George, 174

Painter, Mr., 159, 162
parody, 91
Parton, Dolly, 47
Partridge, Eric, 65
Paycheck, Johnny, 47
People's Temple, 82
Perls, Fritz, 226, 228
Perot, Ross, 214
Petrucci, Armando, 195
Philbin, Regis, 131
Phillips, Kevin, 115
Picasso, Pablo, 29, 50
Pinker, Steven, 151
Pivot, Bernard, 20, 22
Plutarch, 106
political conventions, 115–117
pornography, 182
Porter, Cole, 48
Post, Emily, 114
Potter, Beatrix, 143
Pound, Ezra, 70
PowerPoint (software), 213–215
prefixes, 30, 31, 66–68, 105, 187, 188
prepositions, 140, 191

presentation software, 213–215
Presley, Elvis, 23, 24, 25, 66
Pride, Charlie, 48
Prince, Ellen, 37
Pritchard, Otto, 32
pronouns, 193–194
Proust, Marcel, 185
psychobabble, 227
public relations, 18–19
public writing, 195–197
Pulitzer, Joseph, 80, 81
punch cards, 131–133
punctuation, 154, 160–162, 184–186
puns and punning, 47–49
Putnam, Robert, 97

Quaid, Randy, 64
Quayle, Dan, 55, 56

racism in language,16–17, 45, 94–96, 119
radio programs, 13–15
Randall, Tony, 33
Raspberry, William, 119
reading, 143–145
Reagan, Ronald, 130
Reno, Janet, 14
Republican Party, 115, 116
Reynolds, Malvina, 70, 71
Rialto (Venice, Italy), 176, 177
Ritt, Martin, 70
Roth, Philip, 160, 162
Rowe, Peter, 72
Rozema, Patricia, 92
Ruff, Charles, 123
Rushdie, Salman, 161
Ryan, Nolan, 214

Said, Edward, 110
Sainte-Beuve, Charles, 60

# Word Index